Simply
Healthy
Cooking

Julie Sargent
DN DthD DNMed

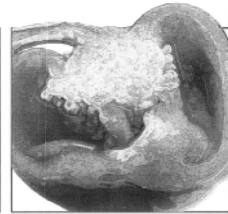

ABOUT THE AUTHOR

I have been in practice as a Nutritional Therapist and Allergy Tester for eight years. Through my work I discovered that people have lost the art and knowledge of how to cook with basic ingredients. We lead hectic lives these days and people often say that they haven't got the time to cook. Hence these day-to-day, quick, healthy and simple recipes for all the family.

Our health is the most important gift we have and to preserve and build on this, we need to prepare meals from natural ingredients.

For some time I have been asked, by many people, to write a book, I'm pleased to say that it is here at last.

I hope you enjoy the recipes as much as we have.

ACKNOWLEDGEMENTS

I would like to thank my children, Charlene and Drew for sampling some good and some not so good meals over the years, thanks guys!

To my husband Phil for his support and encouragement.
To my wonderful granddaughter Rhea, who has inspired me with her enthusiasm.

My grateful thanks to all the people who have helped, encouraged and advised me.

I hope you enjoy using this book as much as I have writing it.

CONTENTS

CONVERSION TABLES

OVEN TEMPERATURES

	° Centigrade	° Fahrenheit	Gas Mark
Very cool	110	225	°
	120	250	1/2
Cool	140	275	1
	150	300	2
Moderate	160	325	3
	180	350	4
Moderately Hot	190	375	5
Hot	200	400	6
	220	425	7
Very Hot	230	450	8

LIQUID MEASURES

4fl oz = 100ml	2 pints = 1.2 litres
$1/4$ pint (5fl oz) = 150ml	$2^1/4$ pints = 1.3 litres
8fl oz = 250ml	$2^1/2$ pints = 1.5 litres
$1/2$ pint (10fl oz) = 275ml	$2^3/4$ pints = 1.6 litres
$3/4$ pint (15fl oz) = 450ml	3 pints = 1.75 litres
1 pint (20fl oz) = 570ml	$3^1/2$ pints = 2 litres
$1^1/4$ pints (25floz) = 750ml	4 pints = 2.25 litres
$1^1/2$ pints (30fl oz) = 900ml	$4^1/2$ pints = 2.5 litres
$1^3/4$ pints (35fl oz) = 1 litre	5 pints = 2.75 litres

SOLID MEASURES

		LENGTH
$1/4$ oz = 10g	12oz = 350g	$1/8$ in = 3 mm
$1/2$ oz = 15g	13oz = 375g	$1/4$ in = 5 mm
$3/4$ oz = 20g	14oz = 400g	$1/2$ in = 1 cm
1 oz = 25g	15oz = 425g	$3/4$ in = 2 cm
$1^1/4$ oz = 40g	1lb = 450g	1 in = 2.5 cm
2 oz = 50g	$1^1/4$ lb = 550g	$1^1/2$ in = 4 cm
$2^1/2$ oz = 65g	$1^1/2$ lb = 675g	2 in = 5 cm
3 oz = 75g	$1^3/4$ lb = 800g	$2^1/2$ in = 6 cm
$3^1/2$ oz = 90g	2 lb = 900g	3 in = 7.5 cm
4 oz = 100g	$2^1/4$ lb = 1kg	$3^1/2$ in = 9 cm
$4^1/2$ oz = 120g	$2^1/2$ lb = 1.1kg	4 in = 10 cm
5 oz = 150g	3 lb = 1.3kg	5 in = 12.5 cm
$5^1/2$ oz = 165g	$3^1/2$ lb = 1.5kg	6 in = 15 cm
6 oz = 175g	4 lb = 1.8kg	7 in = 18 cm
$6^1/2$ oz = 185g	$4^1/2$ lb = 2kg	8 in = 20 cm
7 oz = 200g	5 lb = 2.3kg	9 in = 23 cm
$7^1/2$ oz = 215g	6 lb = 2.7kg	10 in = 25 cm
8 oz = 225g	7 lb = 3.1kg	11 in = 28 cm
9 oz = 250g	8 lb = 3.6kg	12 in = 30 cm
10 oz = 275g	9 lb = 4kg	
11 oz = 300g	10 lb = 4.5kg	

My intention in writing this collection of recipes
is to provide the reader with a starting point
to better health.

Healthy eating doesn't mean 'diet';
it does mean exactly what it says!

The aim of the recipes is to show that good
healthy food, in it's preparation and cooking, can
be simple, nutritious, and – most of all – enjoyable.
The basis of all good food is really simple:
BUY LOCAL, BUY FRESH, and, where possible,
BUY ORGANIC.

Finding a source of good food isn't difficult.
We now have farmers' markets, where the
producer sells direct to the customer; we also have
box schemes, where food can be delivered direct
to your door.
Look for a local butcher or fishmonger, where you
can deal direct with the expert, who can also
advise and help with any enquiries.
A good butcher/fishmonger should be able to tell
you the source of his produce.

You owe it to yourself to do the best for your body
if you want to stay healthy. Go on, cook – you'll
love it!

Julie Sargent

Soups

SOUPS

Soups are a great way of using extra vegetables.
You can have chunky soups or you can put them in a blender to make smooth soups.

In the following pages you will find some ideas, but experiment with any vegetables you have, almost anything will go into a soup.

- **Make a soup nice and hearty by adding cooked rice, millet or Quinoa (see the section on grains), or by adding lentils or beans.**

- **Add raw vegetables to soups right at the end, like grated carrot, chopped watercress or parsley. This will enhance the nutrient value of the soup.**

- **Soups are also a great way of getting children to eat more veggies.**

CARROT AND ORANGE SOUP

This soup can be made more filling by having carrot and potato instead of orange. Or you could make carrot and coriander soup, a nice variation.

375g / 12oz carrots grated
1 small onion, finely chopped
1 tbs olive oil
570 ml / 1 pt vegetable stock
Fresh mint (optional)
Juice of 3 oranges
150g / 5oz plain yoghurt

- Heat the oil in a pan, add the carrots and onion, cook very gently until the carrots are soft
- Pour on the stock, add the mint (if used) and leave to simmer for 20 minutes
- Blend or liquidize
- Add the orange juice, season to taste
- Serve hot or cold with yoghurt

BROWN RICE, CARROT AND CELERY SOUP

This is a very nutritious and filling soup. Lovely on a winters day. It is said that celery helps calm the nerves and is a good anti-inflammatory.

2 carrots grated
4 sticks of celery, diced
1 ltr / 1³/₄pt vegetable stock
2 tbs olive oil
1 medium onion finely chopped
50g / 2oz brown shortgrain rice, washed and drained
1 tbs fresh parsley chopped

- Put the stock in a pan, add the diced celery and carrot, bring to the boil and simmer until the celery and carrots are soft
- Puree the softened celery and carrot in a food processor or blender
- In a clean pan heat the oil, cook the onion until soft then add the rice, stir well
- Add the celery and carrot puree
- Bring to the boil and simmer until the rice is cooked, (about 35-40 minutes)
- Serve with a sprinkling of parsley or coriander

BEETROOT SOUP

Not only a lovely colour but a great way of using extra beetroot. Beetroot is a good blood cleanser and tonic. It is also said to be good for the digestive system.

500g / 1lb raw beetroot chopped
1 medium onion sliced
2 carrots sliced
2 sticks of celery chopped
1200 ml / 2pts vegetable stock
Lemon juice (optional)
1 - 2 tbs natural yoghurt

- Put the stock, beetroot, carrot, onion and celery into a large saucepan, bring to the boil, reduce the heat and simmer until the vegetables are cooked, about 30 mins
- Blend the soup
- You can then either freeze the soup or return to the pan and add the lemon juice, if used, warm through gently
- Serve with a nice spoonful of natural yoghurt

CARROT LEEK AND GINGER SOUP

Leeks are a good source of potassium. It is said they are a great cleanser and diuretic. They are milder than the onion so many people that can't tolerate onions can tolerate leeks.

2 large leeks finely sliced, including some of the green part
2 large carrots, thinly sliced
1 tbs olive oil
1" piece of fresh ginger root, peeled and grated
900 ml / $1^1/_2$ pt vegetable stock
1 bayleaf
2 tbs natural yoghurt
Fresh coriander chopped

- Heat the oil in a pan, add the leeks and just cook until soft
- Add the carrots, ginger, stock and bayleaf, bring to the boil and simmer for about 30 minutes
- Remove the bayleaf and puree in a blender
- Reheat and serve with a swirl of natural yoghurt and sprinkling of chopped coriander

BEAN AND VEGETABLE SOUP

Any bean can be used in this soup, I'm using butter beans but you could use chick peas, aduki beans, red kidney beans, in fact your favourite or whatever you have in stock.

225g / 8oz cooked butter beans
850 ml / $1^1/_2$ pt vegetable stock
1 tbs olive oil
1 large onion sliced
1 stick celery chopped
2 large carrots diced
2 cloves of garlic crushed (optional)
25g / 1oz rice flour or cornflour
275ml / $^1/_2$ pt milk (cows, goats or soya)
Chopped parsley

TIP:
You can use any vegetable and as many as you like to this soup.

If you are using Soya milk, make sure the soup is cool before adding or warm up the milk first, otherwise it will curdle.

- Saute the onion and garlic in the oil until soft, add the rest of the vegetables and stir for a few minutes
- Add the beans and stock, bring to the boil then simmer until the vegetables are just cooked
- Mix the flour with a little of the milk to a runny paste, add the milk to the soup, then gradually add the paste to the soup, stirring all the time, until it becomes a thicker consistency
- Serve with chopped parsley

THICK LEEK AND POTATO SOUP

This one seems to be everyones favourite. I never peel my potatoes – just give them a good wash as many nutrients are just under the skin including potassium. Potatoes are a good source of B vitamins and fibre.

1tbs olive oil
1 large onion chopped
900g / 2lb potatoes cut into chunks
675g / 1¹/2 lb leeks, sliced
575ml / 1pt vegetable stock

- Heat the oil in a saucepan add the onion and fry gently for 5 minutes
- Add the potatoes and leeks, fry gently for another 5 minutes, stirring often
- Add the stock, bring to the boil, turn down the heat and cover
- Simmer for about 15 minutes until the vegetables are just tender
- Mash some of the potatoes to make the soup thick
- Serve with chopped parsley if desired

TIP:
If the soup is too liquid, boil with the lid off until it becomes the consistency you like.

DAL SOUP

This is a favourite of mine. I have this with either a home made spelt roll, (page 101). Or I take it to work in a flask for lunch. Lentils are a good source of B vitamins.

2tbs olive oil
1 onion chopped
1 - 2 cloves garlic, crushed
¹/2 tsp turmeric
1tsp garam masala
¹/4 tsp ground cumin
2 x 400g / 14oz tinned, chopped tomatoes
175g / 6oz red lentils
2 tsp lemon juice
570 ml / 1pt vegetable stock
275 ml / ¹/2 pt coconut milk
Chopped coriander (optional)

- Saute the onion and garlic in the olive oil for 2-3 minutes, add the spices and cook for a half minute
- Stir in the tomatoes, lentils, lemon juice, stock and coconut milk
- Bring to the boil, then reduce the heat and simmer until the lentils are soft, (about 20-30 minutes)
- Garnish with chopped coriander if desired

CURRIED PARSNIP SOUP

When they are in season we can get rather a lot of parsnips,
this is one excellent and tasty way of using them.

1 tbs olive oil
1 onion chopped
1 - 2 cloves garlic, crushed
3 parsnips chopped
1 tbs flour
2 tsp garam masala
$1/2$ tsp chilli powder
900 ml / $1^1/2$ pts vegetable stock
1 lemon, rind and juice

- Saute the onion, parsnips and garlic until just softened,
  about 6 minutes. Stir in the garam masala and chilli
- Sprinkle in the flour mixing well and cook for about half a minute
- Stir in the stock, lemon rind & juice, bring to the boil, then
  reduce the heat to a simmer until the parsnips are just tender,
  (about 20 minutes)
- Blend the soup in a liquidizer.
- Re-heat when ready

TIP:
The best way to peel a pumpkin is to cut it into smaller pieces, then on a chopping board slice off the skin.

PUMPKIN SOUP

As well as a wonderful taste, pumpkins are a rich source of beta-carotene, a nutrient that helps to protect us from cancer.

1kg / 2lb 4oz pumpkin or butternut squash
45g / $1^1/2$ oz butter
1 onion sliced thinly
1 clove of garlic crushed
900 ml / $1^1/2$ pts vegetable stock
$1/2$ tsp ground ginger
1tbs lemon juice
275 ml / $1/2$ pt milk

- Peel the pumpkin, remove the seeds and cut into cubes
- Melt the butter in a large saucepan and sauté the onion and garlic until soft
- Add the pumpkin and stir for a few minutes
- Add the stock, ginger, lemon juice and bring to the boil, then reduce the heat to a simmer
- Cover the pan, cook until the pumpkin is soft
- Blend the soup in a liquidizer
- Stir in the milk and warm through
- You can garnish the soup with a spoon of natural live yoghurt, or single cream

BUTTER BEAN AND TOMATO SOUP
Very quick soup

350g / 12oz cooked butter beans
2 onions chopped
1 bayleaf
1 tbs olive oil
2 x 400g tinned chopped tomatoes
Salt and pepper

- Sauté the onions in the olive oil, until soft, add the tomatoes, butter beans and bayleaf
- Bring to the boil and then simmer for about 10 minutes
- Take out the bayleaf
- Add salt and pepper to taste

This soup can be served as it is, or blended to make a thick soup.

LETTUCE SOUP

Large lettuce shredded
1 onion sliced
25g / 1oz butter
2 tbs flour, (rice, spelt or corn flour)
450ml / 3/4 pt chicken or vegetable stock
450ml/ 3/4 pt milk (organic milk, goats milk or soya milk)
Salt and pepper

- In a saucepan, sauté the onion in the butter for a few minutes
- Add the lettuce, cook for a few minutes
- Stir in the flour
- Gradually add the stock and milk, stirring all the time
  (if using Soya milk, warm the milk before adding to
  the hot lettuce or it will curdle)
- Simmer gently with the lid on for about 20 minutes
- Liquidize

Meat

MEAT

Quality meat is a good source of protein and iron.

- **Buy your meat from local butchers, farms or farmers markets, so that the original source can be identified. The difference in taste is remarkable.**

- **Try using game. Game is naturally reared, without the use of intensive systems. Local suppliers will be able to give you advice on how best to cook them.**

- **Get quality sausages and freeze them, they may seem more expensive, but they are so satisfying that you can't eat many.**

  You can get well made sausages without wheat or gluten. Some local butchers will make them especially for you.

- **Slow cookers are excellent way of cooking meat and vegetables. All you have to do when you get home from work is steam some extra vegetables, which takes minutes.**

- **When cooking casseroles use dry cider or red wine, for an extra special flavour.**

Through my work as a Nutritional Therapist, I found most people know how to cook meat, but needed ideas to be able to get away from the processed meat meals.

COLD SLICED MEAT

Instead of using the sliced processed meats try doing your own.

- Buy whole ham, chicken, beef, or pork
- Cook them in the oven
- Cool them as quickly as possible, by covering and put in a cool place on a wire rack (to allow the air to circulate around the meat). Cool to less than 10°C in $1^1/2$ hours
- You can speed up the cooling time by cutting larger pieces of meat in half, or by cutting the legs off chickens or turkeys

- Once cooled, slice the meat and place between greaseproof paper
- Put into a freezer bag, (write the date you freeze the meat on the bag)
- When you want to use it, take the amount needed out of the freezer and defrost in the fridge

TIP:
• Make sure the meat is firmly pressed together, otherwise they tend to fall apart during cooking.
• You can freeze the burgers before cooking, so make extra. (Don't do this if the meat has been previously frozen.)
• You can use minced chicken, lamb or turkey.
• They can be cooked in the oven, grill or barbeque.

BEEF BURGERS   *Makes about 4 burgers*

450g / 1lb good minced beef
1 small onion finely chopped
$1/2$ tsp of dried mixed herbs,
     or 2 tbs chopped fresh herbs for example:
     parsley, thyme, rosemary.
Olive oil
Salt and pepper
Garlic crushed (optional)

• In a bowl place the mince, onion, herbs, salt and pepper, and garlic if used
• Mix thoroughly
• Divide into four portions, and form into burger shapes, (the thicker they are the longer they take to cook)
• Heat a little olive oil in a frying pan, and cook the burgers on both sides, until cooked through

CHICKEN NUGGETS

I have left the quantities blank, this way you can use as much
or as little as you need..

Chicken breast cut into small chunks
Egg whisked
Breadcrumbs or oats
Salt and pepper
Olive oil

- Pre-heat the oven to 200°C/Gas 6
- Put the crumbs or oats into a bowl
  with some salt and pepper
- Put the whisked egg into a bowl
- Dip the chicken first into the egg then into the crumbs or
  oats, to coat all sides, place onto a plate
- When all the chicken is coated, place onto a baking sheet
- Drizzle a little olive oil over the pieces (not too much,
  otherwise it will be too greasy)
- Bake in the oven until golden brown and the chicken
  is cooked through, the time will depend on how thick
  the chicken nuggets are.
  Cut one in half to check they are cooked through
- Drain on kitchen paper and serve with homemade chips
  (see page 88) and vegetables
- Organic tomato sauce or mayonnaise is nice to dip them in

MEAT KEBABS   *Serves 4-6*

1kg / 2lb 4oz beef cut into chunks

Marinade:
>**Juice of one lemon**
>**2 tbs olive oil**
>**2 cloves garlic crushed**
>**Few sprigs thyme**

- Put the chunks of beef into the marinade, cover and put in the fridge for a few hours or overnight
- Take the meat out of the marinade and drain off most of the oil
- Put onto skewers leaving a little space between
- Cook in the oven, under the grill or on the barbeque

VARIATION:
- Put quarters of onion, baby tomatoes, chunks of courgette or mushrooms between the beef, prior to cooking
- Serve with vegetables, for example, green beans, roasted tomatoes or peppers (see the section on vegetables), salad, rice or on a bed of mashed squash

LAMB KOFTAS   *Serves 4-6*

1kg / 2lb 4oz minced lamb
1 clove garlic crushed
2 tsp mixed herbs
>**or 2 tbs fresh herbs chopped (thyme, rosemary)**
1 onion finely chopped
Salt and pepper

- Put all the ingredients into a bowl and mix thoroughly
- Take out a small handfuls and form into an oblong shape, making sure the meat is firmly pressed together, (so it doesn't fall apart when cooking)
- Place onto a plate
- Put onto skewers if wished or place right onto a baking sheet.
- Bake in the oven until golden brown, and the koftas are cooked right through
- Drain on kitchen paper and serve with a rich tomato sauce or yoghurt dip (see section on sauces), seasonal vegetables or salad

MEAT BALLS IN TOMATO SAUCE   *Serves 4*

450g / 1 lb minced beef
1 egg beaten
1 onion finely chopped
2 cloves garlic crushed
1 tbs fresh herbs, rosemary, thyme, parsley chopped
**   or 1 tsp dried herbs**
Salt and pepper
1 tbs olive oil
Tomato sauce (page 77)

- Pre-heat oven to 180°C/Gas 4
- Combine all the ingredients together – except the tomato sauce, mixing thoroughly
- Roll into small balls, pressing together well, to ensure they don't fall apart
- Put the olive oil into a frying pan, fry the meat balls, turning them until cooked evenly
- Take out and drain, put into a baking dish
- Top with the tomato sauce
- Bake in the oven for about 30 - 40 minutes
- Serve with mashed potato, rice or pasta and vegetables

TIP:
Game is low in cholesterol and fat, therefore a good addition to the diet. Game is more readily available now, from good butchers and farmers markets. It is good roasted, in casseroles, stews, burgers, kebabs etc.

VENISON STEW WITH HERB DUMPLINGS

Serves 3-4

675g / 1^1/2 lb diced venison or rabbit
1 onion diced
1 carrot diced
^{1}/4 swede diced
3 medium potatoes diced
1 tsp mixed herbs
570ml / 1pt stock
150ml / ^{1}/4 pt red wine (optional)
1 tbs spelt or corn flour

Dumplings
100g / 4oz self raising flour
50g / 2oz suet
1 tsp dried herbs
water to mix
extra flour for hands and rolling
salt and pepper

- Put the meat, onion, carrot, swede, potatoes, herbs and stock into a large saucepan
- Bring to the boil, reduce the heat and simmer for 40-55 minutes
- Add the dumplings, put the lid on the pan and continue to cook at a rapid simmer for another 20 minutes
- Add the wine
- If you like the stew to be thicker, just mix the spelt or corn flour to a thin paste with a little water and add to the stew, stirring (being careful not to break the dumplings) until the stew thickens

To make the dumplings:
- Put the flour, suet, salt, pepper and herbs into a bowl and mix
- Add enough water to make a firm dough
- Flour your hands and form the dough into balls, then roll the balls into flour

COTTAGE PIE   *Serves 4*

350g / 12oz minced beef
2 onions chopped
1 tbs olive oil
570ml / 1pt stock
1 tbs fresh herbs sage, thyme, rosemary, chopped
  or 1 - 2 tsp dried mixed herbs
1 tbs spelt, corn or rice flour
450g / 1lb potatoes chopped

- Pre-heat the oven to 190°C/Gas 5
- Boil the potatoes
- Gently sauté the mince in a dry frying pan to extract any fat
  (this won't be necessary with good quality mince).
  Drain off any fat and place the mince in a bowl
- Saute the onions in a little olive oil, until soft
- Add the mince, stock and herbs to the onions,
  simmer gently until the mince is cooked, season to taste
- Mix the flour with a little water to a soft paste,
  stir into the mince mixture, stirring until thickened
- Drain the potatoes, add a little milk and butter then mash
- Place the mince in a deep baking dish, top with the mashed
  potato, forking this neatly onto the mince
- Bake in the oven until the meat is heated through and
  the potato is brown
- Serve with steamed seasonal vegetables

Variations:
- **Instead of stock, use tinned tomatoes**
- **Put grated cheese onto the potatoes before baking
  in the oven**
- **Use any minced meat, chicken, lamb, turkey**

TIP:
If the mince is fatty, gently sauté in a dry frying pan first, drain off the fat and continue as the recipe.

SPAGHETTI BOLOGNAISE *Serves 4*

1 tbs olive oil
2 cloves garlic crushed
1 -2 onions finely chopped
100g / 4oz mushrooms sliced
1 - 2 carrots grated
175g - 225g / 6 - 8oz minced beef
1 x 400g / 14oz tinned chopped tomatoes
1 tbs tomato puree
275ml / $^1/_2$ pt vegetable stock
2 tsp dried oregano or 1 tbs fresh oregano
1 glass red wine (optional)
salt and pepper
225g / 8oz spaghetti
100g / 4oz grated parmesan cheese

- Saute the onion and meat gently for a few minutes, until the onion is just soft
- Add the mushrooms, garlic, carrot and dried herbs if used, sauté for a few minutes
- Add the tomatoes, puree, stock, fresh herbs (if used) and wine (if used), simmer until the sauce has thickened
- Test for flavour, adding salt and pepper if needed
- Cook the spaghetti, when cooked drain and place onto plates, top with the bolognaise and grated parmesan

Variation:
- **You can use rice, millet or Quinoa instead of pasta**

SAUSAGE CASSEROLE   *Serves 4*

Use good quality sausages from farmers markets, local butchers or local farms.

8 sausages
1 - 2 onions chopped
2 carrots chopped or grated
100g / 4oz mushrooms sliced
100g / 4oz cabbage shredded
1 x 400g / 14oz tinned chopped tomatoes
1 tbs tomato puree
5 floz/ $^{1}/_{4}$ pt vegetable stock
1 tbs olive oil
Salt and pepper
1 tbs fresh sage, rosemary, thyme chopped (optional)

- Pre heat oven to 180°C / Gas 4
- Sauté the sausages in the olive oil, turning until they are brown all over
- Take the sausages out and place into a casserole dish.
- Add the onions, carrots, mushrooms, cabbage, tomatoes, puree, stock and herbs (if used)
- Put the lid on the dish and bake for about 40 minutes, until the sausage are cooked through
- Thicken if needed by – mixing 1tbs flour with a little water to a paste and stir into the casserole
- Serve with green vegetables and potatoes

Variation:
- **Instead of tomatoes use 450ml/ $^{3}/_{4}$ pt vegetable stock,**
- **Add more vegetables to the casserole for example, swede, parsnips, squash, cauliflower florets, broccoli florets**

TIP:
To speed up the cooking time, after browning the sausages cut them into halves or quarters.

CHICKEN SUPREME   *Serves 4-6*

1 chicken or 4 - 6 chicken pieces
50g / 2oz butter or margarine
50g / 2oz flour (rice, corn or spelt)
275ml / $^1/_2$ pt chicken or vegetable stock
275ml/ $^1/_2$ pt milk (goats, cows or soya)
100g / 4oz mushrooms sliced
Salt and pepper

- Pre heat oven to 190°C / Gas 5
- Cook the chicken
- While the chicken is cooking make the sauce
- Heat the butter in a saucepan, stir in the flour and cook for a few minutes, stirring all the time
- Gradually stir in the chicken stock and milk, heat until thickened
- Add the mushrooms if used, salt and pepper to taste
- Cook gently until the mushrooms are softened
- Put the sauce to one side
- When the chicken is cooked, take the meat off the bone and place into a casserole dish
- Top with the sauce, stir to combine, place in the oven until heated through – about 10-15 minutes
- Serve with rice and vegetables

CASSEROLE *Serves 4*

2 tbs olive oil
450g / 1lb diced meat, lamb, beef, turkey, chicken, game
Flour (spelt or rice)
Salt and pepper
2 onions chopped or 8 - 12 shallots peeled
3 carrots diced
$^1/_2$ - 1 turnip diced
1 - 2 parsnips diced
570ml / 1pt vegetable stock
1 tbs flour
Salt and pepper

- Pre-heat the oven to 180°C/Gas 4
- Put some flour onto a plate and season with salt and pepper
- Toss the meat into the seasoned flour until coated
- Heat the oil in a frying pan, sauté the meat until the outside is just browned
- Take the meat out and place into a casserole dish
- Add the onions or whole shallots, carrots, turnip, parsnips and stock, give a stir to combine
- Place the lid onto the dish and bake in the oven for about 40-50 minutes, until the meat is just tender
- Thicken the casserole if needed with flour mixed with a little water to a paste, stir into the casserole
- Serve with green vegetables and potatoes

Fish

FISH

A regular query I have is what can be done with fish.
I hope to help you with this in the next few pages.

- **Fish can be bought fresh (then frozen if desired), frozen or tinned.**

- **If you can get to a fish monger he will help you choose the right fish, he will also let you know the best buys – he is the expert.**

- **Fish is very good for you, the oily fish, sardines, mackerel, tuna, herrings, salmon are all high in omega 3 essential fats.**

- **Fish is easier to digest than meat.**

- **Remember fresh is best.**

Coatings for Fish

NUT COATING

- Grind almonds so you have some pieces that are still chunky
- Put some of the ground almonds onto a plate
- Wipe the fish with olive oil
- Put the fish onto the ground nuts then turn the fish over to coat both sides
- Put the fish onto a baking sheet
- When you have coated all the pieces you need, bake in the oven 190°C / Gas 5 until the fish is cooked

> **TIP:**
> **You can grind extra almonds and keep in a jar in the fridge for up to a week.**

FLOUR COATING

You can use spelt flour, rice flour or corn flour.

- Put flour onto a plate and season with salt and freshly ground black pepper
- Coat both sides of the fish in the seasoned flour
- Heat some olive oil in a frying pan and sauté the fish on both sides until cooked
- If the fish is very chunky, sauté both sides then finish off the cooking in the oven on a baking sheet

BAKED IN FOIL

Below are some fish that I would use for this recipe, but that doesn't mean these are the only fish you can use.

Tuna steak, cod, merlin, hake
Olive oil
Lemon or lime juice
Coriander chopped or herbs of your choice
Garlic clove crushed

- Put the fish into foil, making sure you have enough foil to cover the fish. You can do this individually or all together

- On each side of the fish, drizzle olive oil, squeeze of lemon or lime juice, a little crushed garlic and some chopped coriander.
- Fold over the foil to seal the fish inside
- Bake in a moderate oven about 190°C/Gas 5 until cooked, depending on the thickness of the fish
- Fish is cooked when it loses the opaque look

BAKED FISH

Just bake fish in the oven, don't over cook or it will become dry. This could be served with some vegetables for example:
   Sauted carrot and parsnip see page 82.
   Roasted tomatoes see page 83.
   Baby roasted potatoes in olive oil and a sprinkling of sea salt with steamed vegetables.

Mackerel are lovely stuffed with slices of lemon and baked in the oven – this takes away some of the oily taste.

FISH KEBABS *Serves 2-4*

Marinade:
    Olive oil
    Lemon juice
    Crushed garlic
    Herbs of your choice, I love coriander

Chunks of fish (the fishmonger will advise you)
Red and yellow peppers cut into chunks
Baby tomatoes
Courgettes cut into slices
Red onion cut into thick chunks
Small mushrooms

- Marinade the fish for a few hours in the fridge
- Remove the fish from the marinade and place on a plate
- Save the marinade
- Put the vegetables and fish onto skewers alternating them
- Put the kebabs onto a baking sheet and wipe with
  the marinade (I use a pastry brush reserved for this)

You can cook them under the grill, in the oven or of course
on the barbeque.
Lovely with a nice salad or on a plate of cooked rice.

MUSTARD MACKEREL

Mackerel fillets
Olive oil
Dijon mustard

- Score each mackerel about three times on each side
- Brush with oil
- Put a little Dijon mustard into each slit
- Either cook under the grill or wrap in foil & bake in the oven
  190°C/Gas 5 for about 15 minutes depending on the size
- The mackerel is cooked when the centre bone comes away
  from the flesh easily

TIP:
You can thicken the sauce with cornflour if wished.

THAI TUNA

This is a very quick and tasty way to have tuna. You could make enough sauce to have with rice the next day.

Tuna steaks
Coriander, chopped
Lime juice to taste
1 - 2 cloves garlic crushed
Red chilli finely chopped
**   (you can vary this as to how hot you like it)**
1 tin unsweetened coconut milk
Salt and pepper

- Put the tuna into foil and bake in the oven 190°C/gas 5 for about 15 minutes, longer if you have thick steaks
- Put a half to a whole tin of coconut milk into a frying pan, depending on how much sauce you need, add the coriander, lime juice, garlic, chilli, salt and pepper to taste
- Let this simmer for about 5-10 minutes
- Remove the tuna and place on a plate, then pour over the sauce

This would be lovely served with lightly steamed broccoli, sauted grated carrots, or salad.

TIP:
These herring cakes are lovely as a breakfast with just grilled tomato and with scrambled eggs. Also as a lunch with salad.

HERRING CAKES

One herring will make about two cakes. So calculate one herring per person. If the herrings haven't been frozen, you can make a batch of these and freeze them.

1 herring, gutted
1 dessertspoon chick pea flour
Salt and pepper
Olive oil

- Cook the herring either by steaming in a little water or in foil in the oven
- Take off all the flesh, removing the bigger bones and place in a bowl. With a fork, mix the flesh with chick pea flour, salt and pepper
- Form into little patties; you might need to put some chick pea flour onto the outside of the patties if too sticky
- Either freeze or cook in a little olive oil in a shallow frying pan

FISH CAKES *Serves 4*

These can be made very simply or you can be more ambitious
Here is the simple version first.

450g / 1lb potatoes diced
Large tin of salmon – drained
Chopped parsley
Salt and pepper
Olive oil
100g / 4oz breadcrumbs

- Cook the potatoes until tender
- Drain the potatoes and place into a large mixing bowl
- Mash the potatoes
- Add the tinned salmon, parsley and seasoning to taste.
- Stir to combine
- Form into cakes
- You can then either just coat the outside with flour or you can put the fish cake into whisked egg, then coat with oats, sesame seeds or breadcrumbs
- Heat the oil in a shallow frying pan and cook the fish cakes on both sides until heated right through

FISH CAKES – SECOND VERSION *Serves 4-6*

450g / 1lb fresh salmon
450g / 1lb potatoes – diced
Dill chopped
1 onion chopped finely
Olive oil
Juice of lemon
Salt and pepper

- Cook potatoes and mash
- Cook the salmon in foil until just cooked, take off the flesh, removing any bones and flake into the mashed potato
- Sauté the onion in the olive oil until soft, then add to the fish and potato, stir to combine
- Add chopped dill, lemon, salt and pepper to taste
- Form into fish cakes, and coat as above

TIP:
You can freeze the fish cakes before cooking You can also add more potato or fish or both depending on how many you want to make.

TIP:
To make the fish cakes richer for a special meal, you can add butter to the potatoes or a little creme fraiche

KEDGEREE *Serves 4-6*

I love this hot as a main meal and cold the next day with a salad.

450g / 1lb naturally smoked haddock
275g / 10oz brown rice
3 eggs hard boiled
Parsley chopped
227 ml / 8 floz creme fraiche
1 bunch spring onions finely chopped
Salt and pepper

- Steam the fish in a little water in a large saucepan for about 5 minutes until just cooked
- Take the fish out of the water onto a plate
- Rinse the rice and put into the fish water, add more water to cover rice
- Cook the rice; it can take about 40 minutes, adding more water if needed, try to get the rice to absorb all the cooking water
- While the rice is cooking flake the fish and remove any bones
- Peel and roughly chop the eggs
- When the rice is cooked drain if necessary, add the fish, eggs, parsley, spring onion, creme fraiche, salt and pepper to taste, mix gently

Serve with a lovely green salad, a tomato and red onion salad or hot vegetables, for example, green beans, broccoli, sautéed carrots or whatever is in season.

FISH PATE

This paté is rather nice as a special paté with the addition of cream, simple but quite impressive taste. You could use fresh salmon, cooked and flaked.

1 tin pink salmon – drained
1 tin tuna – drained
Lemon juice
Breadcrumbs or oats
Cream

- Put the salmon and tuna into a bowl, add lemon juice to taste and mix together
- Add enough breadcrumbs or oats to make into a firm paté
- Add cream to moisten the paté
- Add salt and pepper if needed
- Put into little ramekin dishes and decorate with a little lemon
- This will keep in the fridge for a day.

FISH CURRY

With this recipe I am giving you the basic ingredients. You can add any vegetables, just chop, shred or dice them and add after you have sautéed the onions and spices.

Any fish cooked and flaked
Onions chopped
About 1 tsp each of: cumin
coriander ground or seeds
turmeric
garam masala
chilli to taste
2 cloves garlic crushed
1 - 2 tins of chopped tomatoes
1 tbs tomato puree
1 tsp bouillon or stock cube

- Sauté the onions, garlic and spices in olive oil until the onions are soft
- Add the vegetables of your choice and cook for a few minutes.
- Add the tomatoes, tomato puree, bouillon, and water if needed
- Cook until the vegetables are just tender
- Add the fish and heat through thoroughly
- Thicken if needed with either corn flour or rice flour, (mix to a paste with cold water, add to the mixture stirring all the time until thickened)

TIP:
Instead of tinned tomatoes and tomato puree you can use coconut milk or you can use water and bouillon as a stock base.

TIP:
Save time by
using a food
processor to
chop/slice the
vegetables.

FISH OR PRAWN STIR FRY *Serves 4*

Very simple meal, use any vegetables in season and any fish. For example:

**Carrots sliced
Peppers sliced
Celery diced
Onions or leeks chopped
Courgettes sliced
Cauliflower cut into florets
Broccoli cut into florets
Parsnips sliced lengthways
Fish of your choice ie: salmon, cod, haddock, tuna
2 cloves garlic crushed
Olive oil
Flavour with either some bouillon, Tamari or Soy sauce
Grated ginger**

- Cook the fish in foil in the oven
- While the fish is cooking sauté the vegetables in olive oil in a large deep frying pan or a wok with either the bouillon, Tamari or Soy sauce and the ginger until the vegetables are just tender
- Take out the fish when cooked and flake or cut into chunks
- Add the fish to the vegetables and serve. If using cooked prawns add just at the end to heat through thoroughly

COATING FOR SALMON *Serves 2-4*

This could also be used for tuna steaks

**Salmon fillets cut into strips lengthways, keep skin on
Clove garlic crushed
2.5cm / 1" fresh ginger grated
4 spring onion chopped
Grated zest and juice of 1/2 a lemon
1 - 2 tbs runny honey
1 tbs soy sauce**

- Mix together in a food processor the garlic, ginger, onion, zest and juice of the lemon, honey and soy sauce
- Check for flavour adding more honey, soy sauce or lemon juice as to your taste
- Brush the salmon steaks with the mixture
- Bake under a hot grill or on a griddle, until cooked, this will only take a few minutes

TUNA AU-GRATIN *Serves 4*

1 x large tin tuna, drained
1 onion chopped
1 clove garlic crushed
2 sticks celery finely chopped
1 red pepper diced
1 yellow pepper diced
1 -2 carrots grated
100g / 4oz mushrooms sliced
1 - 2 tbs olive oil
2 tbs parsley chopped
175g / 6oz pasta
570ml / 1 pt cheese sauce (page 72)
100g / 4oz breadcrumbs
50g / 2oz grated cheese

- Pre-heat the oven to 180°C/gas 4
- Cook the pasta, and drain in a colander
- Sauté the onion, garlic, celery, peppers, grated carrot and mushrooms until just softened slightly
- Put the drained pasta into an oven proof dish; add the sautéed vegetables, tuna and the cheese sauce, mix altogether
- Cover with the breadcrumbs and a little grated cheese
- Bake in the oven until heated right through and crispy on the top, about 20-30 minutes

FISH PIE *Serves 4*

450g / 1lb white fish cod, haddock, coley etc
570ml / 1pt milk (cows, goats or soya)
100g / 4oz mushrooms sliced
2 onions finely chopped
1 tbs olive oil or butter
2 tbs parsley chopped
900g / 2 lb potatoes
Salt and pepper
50g / 2oz flour (rice, spelt or corn)

- Pre heat the oven to 190°C/Gas 5
- Put the milk into a saucepan, add the fish and cook gently until the fish is just cooked
- Cook the potatoes
- Take the fish out of the milk, keeping the milk to make the sauce
- Bone the fish and leave to one side
- Sauté the onions in a little butter or olive oil until soft
- Make the white sauce (page 71) using 50g/2oz flour and milk from cooking the fish, taste for flavour adding more salt and pepper if needed
- Mash the potatoes with a little milk
- Place the fish, mushrooms, onions and parsley in a deep baking dish, cover with the white sauce, stir to combine
- Top with the mashed potato, forking it over
- Either top with a little grated cheese or dotted with a little butter
- Bake in the oven for about 30 minutes until heated through and the potato is slightly browned
- Serve with green vegetables and carrots or vegetables of your choice

Variations:
- **Add chopped hard boiled eggs to the white sauce before topping with potatoes**
- **Add cooked prawns as above**
- **Use natural smoked haddock instead of white fish or combine the both**

Vegetarian
Meals

VEGETARIAN MEALS

For too many people, the prospect of cooking a vegetarian meal can be daunting, due to the belief that they need to spend hours soaking, and cooking beans, and then are not completely sure what to do with them.
My aim is to eliminate this belief and show that bulk soaking, cooking and freezing will make the recipes, quick and easy.

Pulses, lentils and beans are rich in protein, minerals and fibre, rich in B complex and very low in fat.
They are complex carbohydrates, helping to keep sugar balance even.
When combined with a grain they have all eight essential amino acids, ensuring good protein.

They make filling, nutritious and cheap meals.

FREEZING BEANS

The only beans I don't pre-freeze are red kidney beans;
I always buy these in a tin because they contain a toxin that can be poisonous if not cooked properly.

Pre-freeze any other bean; chick pea, butter bean, adzuki bean, haricot etc. I usually have two types in the freezer at one time and vary which ones I freeze.

Adding seaweed to the cooking water helps eliminate flatulence.

- **Soak the whole bag of organic dried beans in lots of water overnight**
- **Drain and rinse**
- **Put into a saucepan and cover with water, adding seaweed (optional)**
- **Bring to the boil, reduce the heat and simmer until just soft**
- **This can range from $1/2$ hr to $1^1/2$ hrs, depending on the bean**
- **When cooked, drain and cool, (you can cool them quickly by running the beans under cold water)**
- **Put them onto a baking sheet and freeze**
- **When frozen, remove the beans from the tray, using a spatula and put into a freezer bag**
- **You then have free flow beans**

When using frozen beans in a recipe, ensure they are heated thoroughly.
If you are using them in a salad, defrost in the fridge overnight.

LOAVES

These loaves can be made, sliced and frozen.
They are nice hot with gravy and vegetables or cold next day
with salad and chutney or cranberry sauce, see page 75.

NUT LOAF   *Serves 4*

Any nut can be used in this recipe or a combination of nuts,
to give a different flavour.

2 onions chopped
1 tbs olive oil
225g / 8oz mixed nuts roughly chopped
1 heaped tablespoon flour (spelt, rice or corn flour)
1 egg beaten
275ml / ¹/2 pt vegetable stock
75g / 3oz spelt breadcrumbs or oats
Salt and pepper

- Pre-heat the oven to 190°C / Gas 5
- Sauté the onions in the oil until soft
- Add the flour, cook for a couple of minutes
- Add the stock and cook until thickened – stirring all the time
- Remove from the heat; mix in the egg, nuts and breadcrumbs
  or oats
- Add salt and pepper if needed
- Put into a greased loaf tin, and cover with foil
- Bake in the oven for about 45 minutes

Variations:
- **Put half the nut mixture into the loaf tin, then
  a layer of sliced tomatoes, or roasted peppers,
  then the rest of the nut mixture**
- **Put small chunks of soft goat's cheese, halloumi or
  buffalo cheese in the middle of the nut mixture**
- **Grated carrot in the middle, gives it a great colour
  when sliced**

RED LENTIL LOAF   *Serves 4*

225g / 8oz red lentils
450ml / ³/4pt vegetable stock
1 onion finely chopped
1 tbs olive oil
1 egg beaten
125g / 4oz grated cheese (optional)
1 tbs lemon juice
25g / 1oz spelt breadcrumbs or oats
Salt and pepper

- Pre-heat the oven to 190°C / gas5
- Put the lentils and stock into a saucepan, bring to the boil then reduce the heat to simmer with the lid off, until soft and all the liquid has been absorbed, (about 20 minutes)
- Sauté the onions in olive oil until soft
- Add the cooked lentils, lemon juice, beaten egg, and cheese (if used)
- The mixture needs to be stiff, add breadcrumbs or oats if the mixture is too soft
- Put into grease loaf tin, cover with foil and bake in the oven for about 35 minutes
- Remove the foil and continue cooking for a further 10 minutes, to crisp the top

TIP:
Ensure the lentils
absorb all the
cooking water;
they need to be
quite dry before
mashing them.

GREEN LENTIL LOAF   *Serves 4-6*

Green lentils take longer to cook than red. To speed up the cooking process, either soak overnight in water or put into a bowl and pour boiling water over them, leave to soak for 10-15 minutes, then drain.

350g / 12oz green lentils cooked
2 onions chopped
1 carrot grated
1 tsp cumin
1 tsp coriander
1 tsp turmeric
Fresh lemon juice
1 clove garlic crushed
Salt and pepper
1tbs olive oil

- Pre-heat the oven to 180°C/Gas 4
- Sauté the onion, spices, garlic and carrot in the olive oil, until soft
- Mash the lentils with a potato masher or in a food processor
- Mix the lentils with the onion mixture
- Add salt, pepper and lemon juice to taste
- Put the mixture into a greased loaf tin and cover with foil
- Bake in the oven until heated through, about 30 minutes

BURGERS
Making and Freezing Burgers

QUICK RED LENTIL BURGERS

350g / 12oz red lentils
750ml / $1^1/_4$ pts water
$1/_2$ - 1 tsp vegetable bouillon or stock cube
1 onion finely chopped
1 egg beaten
Breadcrumbs or oats
Olive oil

- Cook the lentils in the water and stock until soft
  and all the water has been absorbed, (about 20 minutes)
- Leave to cool
- Sauté the onion in the olive oil until soft
- Add the lentils and mix until all combined
- Form into burger shapes
- Coat the burger in egg, then in breadcrumbs or oats
- Cook in a little olive oil in a frying pan or in the oven,
  or freeze at this stage

Variation:
- **Add tomato puree to the lentil mixture**
- **When sautéing the onion add spices, cumin, coriander,
  chilli, turmeric.**
- **Add herbs or parsley to the mixture before making into burgers.**

LENTIL BURGERS

350g / 12oz brown lentils
900ml / 1^1/$_2$ pts water
^{1}/$_2$ - 1 tsp vegetable bouillon
2 tbs olive oil
2 onions finely chopped
2 - 4 cloves garlic crushed
175g / 6oz spelt breadcrumbs, oats or sesame seeds
plus extra for coating

- Cook the lentils in the water and stock unit soft
  and all the liquid has been absorbed, about 30 minutes
- Sauté the onion and garlic, until the onions are soft
- Remove from the heat, add the lentils and breadcrumbs or oats,
  mix well
- Form into burger shapes
- Coat with the breadcrumbs, oats, or sesame seeds
- Either freeze or cook in a little olive oil in a frying pan,
  or on a baking sheet in the oven

RED BEAN BURGER

2 x 245g tins red kidney beans, drained and rinsed
2 onions finely chopped
2 tbs chopped parsley
1 tbs olive oil
1 - 2 cloves garlic crushed
100g / 4oz soft goat's cheese or Halloumi cheese
1 - 2 eggs whisked
Breadcrumbs or oats

- Sauté the onion and garlic in the olive oil, until soft
- In a food processor put the beans, onions, and parsley, blend
  until most of the beans are mushy but leaving some larger pieces
  (or use a potato masher)
- If the mixture is too soft to make into burgers,
  add breadcrumbs or oats to thicken
- Form into burgers, placing a piece of cheese
  in the centre of each one
- Dip the burger into the whisked egg, then into the breadcrumbs
  or oats (You can freeze at this stage)
- Cook in a little olive oil in a frying pan or in the oven
  on a baking sheet until heated through

VEGETABLE CRUMBLE   *Serves 4-6*

2 carrots diced
1 head of broccoli cut into florets
1 parsnip diced
1 - 2 leeks sliced
$^1/_2$ - 1 cauliflower cut into florets
50g / 2oz corn flour, rice flour, or spelt flour
$^1/_2$ - 1 tsp vegetable bouillon
570ml / 1pt white sauce (page 71)

Topping:
100g / 4oz rice flour
100g / 4oz porridge oats
100g / 4oz margarine or butter
Salt and pepper

- Pre-heat the oven to 190°C/Gas 5
- Very lightly steam the vegetables; they should be
  just under cooked
- Put the vegetables into a deep baking dish
- Cover the vegetables with the white sauce, give a stir
- Make the crumble; put the rice flour and the oats into
  a basin, dice the margarine or butter into the flour mixture,
  and mix with your finger tips, until the mixture resembles
  fine breadcrumbs
- Add salt and pepper
- Cover the vegetables with the crumble mixture
- Bake in the oven for about 20 minutes, or until heated
  right through and the crumble mixture is golden brown

VEGETABLE CASSEROLE   *Serves 2-4*

This is one version, but remember you can use any vegetable in season, with any bean or lentil.

2 potatoes diced
2 carrots diced
1/2 swede diced
2 onions chopped
1 parsnip sliced
Water
1tsp vegetable bouillon
2 bay leaves
Sprig rosemary
225g/8oz cooked butter beans
1tbs corn flour, rice flour or spelt flour

- Pre-heat the oven to 180°C/Gas 4
- Put all the vegetables and the butter beans into a large casserole dish
- Add the bay leaves, rosemary and bouillon
- Pour the water over the vegetables until just covered
- Put the lid on the casserole dish and bake in the oven until the vegetables are just cooked, (about 45-60 minutes)
- Take out the bay leaves
- If the casserole is not thick enough, mix the flour into a loose paste by adding water, and stir into the casserole until thick
- Check for seasoning adding more bouillon, or salt and pepper if needed
- Serve with cabbage or greens

TIP:
- instead of stock you could use tinned tomatoes
- If you have time cook the casserole on a lower heat for longer.

BEAN CASSOULETTE   *Serves 4*

This is a lovely, rich, warming meal for those cold winter nights.

100g / 4oz mushrooms
2 x 400g / 14oz tinned chopped tomatoes
1 x 245g / 9oz tinned red kidney beans, drain and rinse
1 x tin of chestnuts
1 - 2 courgettes sliced
12 shallots peeled
1 tbs tomato puree
$^{1}/_{2}$ - 1 tsp bouillon
2 tbs olive oil

- Pre-heat the oven to 160°C / Gas 3
- Put all the ingredients, except the chestnuts,
  into a large casserole dish, stir well
- Cook in the oven for approximately 1 hour
  adding the chestnuts near the end of cooking
- Check for seasoning
- Serve with potatoes and seasonal vegetables, for example,
  broccoli, cauliflower, squash

CHILLI   *Serves 4*

The easiest chilli you will ever make.

Rich tomato sauce (page 77)
1/2 - 1 tsp of chilli powder or fresh chilli finely chopped
400g / 14oz tinned red kidney beans

- Make the tomato sauce adding the chilli powder
- Drain and rinse the kidney beans, add to the tomato sauce
- Heat through
- Test for flavour adding more chilli or seasoning if needed
- Serve on a bed of steamed vegetables, brown rice, millet,
  or quinoa, and salad

Variation:
- **Add diced carrot, courgette and peppers. Add at the second
  stage of the recipe.**

TIP:
This can be cooled and frozen in handy portions

BAKED BEANS   *Serves 4-6*

This homemade version is low in salt and sugar. The beans give a good source of iron and fibre. The haricot bean is the classic baked bean, but you can use any bean you like.

450g / 1lb cooked haricot beans
2 x 400g / 14oz tinned chopped tomatoes
2 tbs tomato purée
2 tsp brown sugar or black strap molasses
1 large onion finely chopped
Salt and pepper

- Heat the oil in a large pan, sauté the onion until soft
- Add the rest of the ingredients
- Cook until a nice thick consistency, this can be done on top of the stove or in a covered casserole dish in the oven, (180°C/Gas 4, for about 40-60 minutes)

TIP:
This is nice cold the next day with salad.

RICE AND MUSHROOMS   *Serves 4*

The more varied the mushrooms the better this looks and tastes.

350g / 12oz various mushrooms
225g / 8oz brown rice
$1/2$ - 1 tsp bouillon
1 tbs olive oil
1oz butter
450ml / $3/4$ pt water
1 small pot creme fraiche
2 cloves garlic crushed
Salt and pepper

- In a deep frying pan put the olive oil and butter, sauté the mushrooms and the garlic until the mushrooms are just soft
- Remove the mushrooms with a slotted spoon and reserve.
- Put the rice, water, bouillon into the frying pan, bring to the boil, reduce the heat and simmer until the rice is cooked and has absorbed all the water, (about 40 minutes)
- Add the mushrooms
- Stir in the creme fraiche
- Add salt and pepper to taste
- Serve with green salad and tomato salad or steamed seasonal vegetables

STUFFED CABBAGE LEAVES *Serves 2*

Nutmeg goes beautifully with the rice.
You will need about three stuffed leaves per person.

6 large cabbage leaves
1 x 400g / 14oz tinned chopped tomatoes
100g / 4oz brown rice
Whole nutmeg
$^1/_2$ - 1 tsp vegetable bouillon

- Pre-heat the oven to 180°C/Gas 4
- Put the rice into a saucepan and cover with water, add the bouillon, bring to the boil, then reduce the heat and simmer until cooked
- While the rice is cooking, lightly steam the cabbage leaves until just soft
- Cut out the hard centre of each cabbage leaf, keeping the leaf whole
- When the rice is cooked, drain, if it hasn't absorbed all the water
- Grate some nutmeg into the rice, so you can just detect the taste
- Season with salt and pepper if necessary.
- Put a good spoonful of the rice onto each cabbage leaf.
- Fold the bottom of the leaf up over the rice, fold the sides over, then the top of the leaf over them, so you have a parcel, and all the rice is covered
- Put into an oven proof dish, with the folds facing down
- Cover with the tinned tomatoes
- Cover the dish with foil, and bake in the oven for about 30 minutes
- Serve with any vegetables, for example, carrot, squash, cauliflower, potatoes etc

STUFFED MUSHROOMS   *Serves 2*

This is so quick and a favourite of mine.

4 large flat mushrooms
1 large onion finely chopped
100g / 4oz breadcrumbs or oats
1 - 2 cloves garlic crushed
1 dessertspoon olive oil
Lemon juice
Salt and pepper
25 - 50g / 1 - 2oz grated cheese plus extra for topping

- Pre-heat the oven to 180°C / Gas 4
- Cut the stalk out of the mushrooms, and chop
- Sauté the onion and mushroom stalks in the olive oil, until the mushrooms are soft
- Add the breadcrumbs or oats, garlic, and grated cheese, cook for a few minutes
- Add lemon juice, salt and pepper to taste
- Lay the mushrooms on a baking dish, underside facing up
- Put a good spoonful of the mixture onto each mushroom, don't worry if it overflows
- Top with a little more grated cheese
- Bake in the oven until the mushrooms are just cooked, and the topping is golden brown, about 20 minutes

PEPPERS STUFFED WITH RICE   *Serves 2-4*

4 red peppers
225g / 8oz brown rice
1 - 2 onions finely chopped
2 cloves garlic crushed
$^1/_2$ - 1 tsp bouillon
2 celery sticks finely chopped
2 large tomatoes chopped
1 tbs olive oil
250g / 9oz Halloumi cheese
2 tbs parsley chopped

- Pre-heat oven to 190°C/Gas 5
- Blanch the whole peppers by placing in a large saucepan with boiling water, cook for 3-4 minutes, then remove from the hot water, and leave to one side
- Cook the rice with the bouillon about 40 minutes, drain if necessary.
- Sauté the onions, garlic, and celery in the olive oil until soft
- Add the tomatoes to the onion mixture and cook for a few minutes
- Mix the rice and parsley into the tomato mixture, check for flavour adding salt and pepper if needed
- Cut the tops off the peppers and scoop out the seeds, running under water if necessary
- Put the peppers into a baking dish and fill each one with the rice mixture, top with a little Halloumi
- Bake in the oven until the peppers are just cooked, about 20-30 minutes

STUFFED COURGETTE   *Serves 2-4*

4 courgettes cut into half lengthways
Rich tomato sauce (page 77)
175g / 6oz red lentils
250g / 9oz Haloumi cheese or goat's cheese
1 tbs olive oil

- Pre-heat oven to 180°C/Gas 4
- Cook the lentils, (about 20-25 minutes); make sure they absorb all the water.
- Cut out the centre of the courgettes, leaving a shell.
- Finely chop the centres of the courgettes and sauté in olive oil until just soft
- Mix the courgette and the cooked lentils into the tomato mixture
- Put the courgette shells onto a baking sheet and fill each one with the tomato mixture.
- Put a few pieces of cheese onto each one
- Bake in the oven for 30-40 minutes, until the courgettes are tender

BEAN KEBABS   *Serves 4*

400g / 14oz cooked adzuki beans
175g / 6oz millet
450 ml / $^3/_4$ pt vegetable stock
3 tbs olive oil
1 onion finely chopped
2 garlic cloves crushed
2 tbs fresh coriander chopped
1 tsp ground cumin
3 eggs beaten
120g / $4^1/_2$ oz breadcrumbs or oats
Salt and pepper
Wooden skewers
  (soak in water for 20 minutes to prevent burning)

- Cook the millet in the stock until all the stock has been absorbed, (about 20 minutes)
- Sauté the onion, garlic and cumin in the oil until the onions are just soft.
- Into a food processor put the onion mixture, beans, fresh coriander, millet, eggs, salt and pepper to taste
- Blend until just mixed, allow to cool (it becomes firmer when cool)
- Form into oval shapes and put onto a wooden skewer, about three on each one
- Brush with olive oil and grill, turning, so all the sides become golden brown. Serve with a green salad

SCOTCH EGGS   *Serves 2*

2 eggs hard boiled
175g / 6oz red lentils
Rice flour or spelt flour
1/2 tsp bouillon
450ml / ³/4 pt water,
1 egg beaten
Olive oil
Breadcrumbs or oats to coat

- Cook the lentils in the water and bouillon,
  until the lentils are soft and have absorbed all the water
- Leave to cool
- Peel the eggs and roll in the flour
- Press the lentil mixture around the egg, until completely covered
- Roll the scotch egg in the whisked egg,
  then into the breadcrumbs or oats to coat
- Pour olive oil into a deep frying pan,
  so you have about an inch of oil
- Heat the oil, then add the eggs, rolling them so all sides
  become golden brown
- Drain on kitchen paper

REFRIED BEANS   *Serves 4-6*

2 x 400g / 14oz tinned red kidney beans
2 onions finely chopped
3 garlic cloves crushed
¹/2 tsp chilli powder
2 tbs fresh coriander chopped
2 tbs olive oil
150 ml / ¹/4 pt vegetable stock

- Heat the oil in a large frying pan, sauté the onion,
  garlic and chilli until the onions are soft
- Mash the beans with a potato masher, leaving some beans whole
- Stir the mashed beans into the onion mixture, with the coriander
- Stir in the stock and cook the beans, stirring, until they are
  soft and mushy, about 5 minutes, (being careful not to let them
  stick on the bottom, add more stock if they become too dry)
- Then leave to cool
- These beans can be used to stuff pancakes, tortillas or vegetables
- They are also good with garlic bread

FALAFEL

650g / 1 lb 7oz cooked chick peas
1 onion finely chopped
3 cloves of garlic crushed
100g / 4 oz breadcrumbs or oats
1/4 tsp chilli
1 tsp ground turmeric
1 tsp ground coriander
1 tsp ground cumin
1 tbs fresh coriander chopped
Salt and pepper
1 egg beaten
Breadcrumbs or oats to coat
Olive oil

TIP:
These can be cooked and frozen.

- In a food processor put the chick peas, onions, garlic, breadcrumbs, (or oats), chilli, cumin, coriander, turmeric, and fresh coriander
- Blend for a few seconds.
- Add salt and pepper to taste
- Form into small balls
- Put each falafel into the whisked egg then into the breadcrumbs or oats to coat
- Fry them in a little olive until they are golden brown
- Drain on kitchen paper
- Serve hot or cold, nice with tzatziki (page 78) or tomato sauce (page 77)

STUFFED PANCAKES

CHICK PEA MIX   *Fills 4-6 pancakes*

4-6 pancakes (see page 102)
400g / 14oz cooked chick peas
2 cloves garlic crushed
1 tbs rice flour
1 tbs olive oil
2 - 3 tomatoes chopped
$1/2$ - $1/4$ cucumber chopped
3 tbs natural live yoghurt
Salt and pepper

- Put the rice flour onto a plate and season with salt and pepper
- Roll the chick peas in the seasoned flour until they are all coated
- Heat the olive oil in a frying pan
- Take the chick peas out of the flour and put into
  the heated oil, add the garlic
- Cook until golden brown, stirring a few times
- Fold the pancake in half, then half again,
  so you have a triangular shape
- Open one of the folds and fill with some chick peas,
  a few tomatoes and cucumber, and top with some yoghurt

LENTIL FILLING   *Fills 4-6 pancakes*

4-6 pancakes (page 102)
350g / 12oz lentils
750 ml / 1¹/₄ pt vegetable stock
1 onion finely chopped
1 courgette chopped
1 red pepper chopped
1 tbs olive oil
100g / 4oz grated cheese
1pt white sauce (see page 71)

- Pre-heat oven to 180°C/gas 4
- Cook the lentils in the vegetable stock,
  until they are soft and all the water has been absorbed
- Heat the olive oil in a frying pan and sauté the onions,
  courgette and red pepper until just soft.
- Mix the vegetables with the lentils
- Place a good spoonful along the centre of each pancake
  and roll into a sausage shape
- Place into a greased ovenproof dish
- Pour the white sauce over the pancakes
  and top with grated cheese
- Bake in the oven for about 20 minutes, until heated through
  and the cheese has melted and browned
- Serve with steamed seasonal vegetables or salad

REFRIED BEAN FILLING   *Fills 4-6 pancakes*

4-6 pancakes (page 102)
1 x quantity of refried beans (page 52)
Natural yoghurt
2 cloves of garlic crushed

- Pre-heat oven 180°C/Gas 4
- Fill the centre of each pancake with the bean mixture and roll
- Place onto a greased ovenproof dish and cover with foil
- Place in the oven and heat through thoroughly
  (about 15-20 minutes)
- Mix the garlic with the yoghurt
- Place the pancake onto the plate, with a side serving of
  the yoghurt
- Serve with a tomato and basil salad

TIP:
These are ideal frozen and used for packed lunches. Take out of the freezer and defrost in the fridge overnight.

PIZZA   *Serves 4-6*

1 x spelt bread recipe (see page 101)
400g / 14oz tinned chopped tomatoes
1 tbs olive oil
2 cloves garlic crushed
1 onion finely chopped
1 tsp dried oregano, or 1 tablespoon of fresh herbs chopped
1 red pepper sliced
225g / 8oz soft goats cheese, buffalo or Hallumi
1 small tin of anchovies (optional)
Few mushrooms

- Pre heat oven to 220°C/gas 7
- Make the bread recipe. Roll out to a large round or make into flat rolls for individual pizzas. Put onto a baking sheet
- In a frying pan sauté the onion and garlic, until the onions are just soft
- Add the tomatoes, olive oil and dried herbs (if using)
- Cook until the mixture becomes thick
- Take off the heat and add the fresh herbs (if using)
- Put the tomato mixture onto the pizza base, avoid getting too close to the edge
- Top with peppers, mushrooms, anchovies and cheese. (or your favourite toppings for pizza)
- Bake in the oven for about 10 minutes, or until the pizza base is cooked and the cheese is bubbling and brown
- Eat them hot, or leave to go cold and freeze

HUMMUS   *Serves 4*

1 x 400g / 14oz tinned chick peas drained
Juice of 1 lemon
4 tbs tahini (sesame paste, available from health food shops)
2 cloves garlic crushed
salt and pepper
2 tbs olive oil

- Put all the ingredients into a food processor, blend well
  until a smooth paste. You might need to stop the machine
  a few times, to get the mixture away from the sides
- Check for flavour adding more lemon juice, garlic or
  salt and pepper to taste
- Put in a covered dish in the fridge,
  or freeze in small containers

Variation:
- **Use butter beans instead of chick peas.**

GUACAMOLE   *Serves 4-6*

2 ripe avocados
2 tomatoes finely chopped
2tbs lime or lemon juice
1 tbs coriander chopped
little chilli (optional)
salt and pepper

- Peel the avocados, take out the stone
- Spoon the flesh from the avocados into a bowl
- Mash with a fork
- Add the other ingredients and mix well, taste for flavour
  adding more lime juice, coriander, salt and pepper if needed

TIP:
This is good with
- **raw vegetables, carrots, cucumber, celery, tomatoes**
- **make a parcel with large lettuce leaves. Put a spoonful of guacamole in the middle of the leaf, fold the bottom of the leaf up, then the sides over, then the top of the leaf down to make a parcel**
* **Corn chips**
* **Roasted potato wedges (see page 88 as potato chips)**

LENTIL BOLOGNAISE   *Serves 4*

1 large onion chopped
2 tbs olive oil
2 cloves garlic crushed
1 tsp dried oregano or 1 tbs fresh herbs chopped
225g / 8oz spit red lentils
1 x 400g / 14oz tinned chopped tomatoes
450ml / 3/4pt vegetable stock
Salt and pepper

- Saute the onion in the olive oil until soft
- Add the tomatoes, garlic, dried oregano (if using), lentils and water
- Bring to the boil, reduce the heat to simmer until the lentils are soft (about 20 minutes)
- Add fresh herbs (if using)
- Season with salt and pepper
- Serve with cooked rice, pasta or rice noodles

Variation:
- **Add grated carrot at the second stage.**

LENTIL SHEPHERDS PIE   *Serves 4-6*

350g / 12oz red, green or brown lentils
570ml / 1pt vegetable stock
2 onions chopped
1 tbs olive oil
225g / 8oz mushrooms sliced
2 x 400g / 14oz tinned chopped tomatoes
1 tbs tomato puree
1 tsp dried mixed herbs
salt and pepper
450g / 1lb potatoes, cooked and mashed

- Pre-heat oven to 190°C / Gas 5
- In a deep saucepan sauté the onions in olive oil until soft
- Add the lentils, stock, tomatoes, puree and herbs, bring to
  the boil, reduce the heat and simmer until the lentils are cooked
- Take off the heat, add the mushrooms and season to taste
- Place the tomato mixture into a deep baking dish and
  top with the mashed potato, forking neatly on top
- Bake in the oven for about 15 minutes until the potato is brown
- Serve with seasonal vegetables for example,
  greens and cauliflower

MOUSSAKA   *Serves 4-6*

2 carrots diced into small pieces
2 courgettes sliced
2 onions chopped
175g / 6oz mushrooms
1 head of broccoli cut into florets
1 x white sauce (see page 71)
1 x tomato sauce (see page 77)
2 large potatoes

- Pre-heat the oven 190°C / Gas 5
- Steam the potatoes until just tender. Cool and slice
- Mix the vegetables with the tomato sauce
- Put into a deep baking dish
- Cover the tomato mixture with the potatoes,
  slightly overlapping the slices
- Top with the white sauce
- Bake in the oven for about 30 minutes

VEGETABLE COBBLER   *Serves 4-6*

This recipe takes a bit more time, but a lovely meal on a winter's night.

8 pickling onions or shallots
250g / 9oz swede chopped
3 carrots diced
1/2 cauliflower cut into florets
250g / 9oz mushrooms
1 x 400g / 14oz tinned chopped tomatoes
50g / 2oz red lentils
2 tbs spelt or rice flour
1 - 2 cloves garlic crushed
3 - 4 tablespoons water
275 ml / 1/2 pt vegetable stock
2 tbs chopped parsley
1 tbs olive oil
Salt and pepper

Topping:
250g / 9oz spelt flour
1 heaped teaspoon baking powder
50g / 2oz butter diced
salt and pepper
1 egg beaten
150 ml / 1/4 pt milk

- Pre heat the oven 220°C / Gas 7
- Saute the onions, swede, cauliflower, carrots,
  garlic in the olive oil in a deep frying pan for about 5 minutes
- Add the tomatoes, mushrooms, stock and lentils,
  cook until the vegetables are just tender (about 20 minutes)

Make the cobbler:
- Put the flour, baking powder, salt and pepper into a bowl
  and mix
- Rub the butter into the flour with your finger tips, until it
  resembles fine breadcrumbs.
- Add the beaten egg and enough milk to make a dough,
  and knead until the mixture comes away from the bowl
- Roll on a floured surface to 1cm / 1/2" thick.
- Cut into 5cm / 2" rounds

- Thicken the vegetable mixture by mixing the spelt

or rice flour with a little water to a soft paste,
stir into the vegetables
- Heat until thickened.
- Add salt and pepper to taste
- Put the vegetables into an oven proof dish
- Place the scones on top of the vegetables, brush with beaten egg
- Bake in the oven for 10-12 minutes, until the scones are cooked and golden brown

TOFU

It is a soya bean curd. It doesn't have any flavour as such,
so it allows you to add flavour. Below are some simple recipes:

TOFU BURGERS   *Makes 3-4 burgers*

1 block organic tofu
1 onion finely chopped
1 clove garlic crushed
1 tbs chopped herbs of your choice
$^1/_2$ - 1 tsp bouillon
1 tbs olive oil

- Pre-heat the oven 180°C/Gas 4
- Sauté onions in olive oil until soft, add the garlic and cook for a minute
- In a food processor put the tofu, herbs, bouillon and onion
- Blend for a short time (you don't want it to go too soft)
- Flour your hands, form the tofu into round burgers
- Wipe a little olive oil on both sides of the burgers
- Put onto a baking sheet and bake in the oven until heated through, about 10-15 minutes

MARINADED TOFU   *Serves 2-3*

1 block organic tofu
1 tbs olive oil
1 tbs soy sauce
small piece of fresh ginger grated
1 - 2 cloves garlic crushed

- Cut the tofu into chunks
- Put all the other ingredients into a deep bowl, mix together
- Put the tofu into the marinade
- Cover and put into the fridge for a few hours
- Take the tofu out of the marinade
- Stir fry with vegetables

CRISPY TOFU   *Serves 2-3*

This is nice served hot with stir fried vegetables or cold on salads.

1 block organic tofu
3 tbs rice flour
$1/4$ tsp of each; ground cumin, garam masala,
  coriander, turmeric
salt and pepper
olive oil

- Slice the tofu to the thickness of your choice
- In a bowl, mix the flour, spices, salt and pepper
- Coat each side of the tofu with the flour
- Heat the olive oil in a frying pan
- Saute the tofu on both sides, until crispy
- Serve on a salad, or add to stir fried or roasted vegetables

ROULADE   *Serves 6*

Very impressive dish, your family and friends will think you have spent hours on this, only you and I know it didn't take long and is quite easy.

4 eggs separated
75g / 3oz cheddar cheese grated
50g / 2oz cottage cheese
1/2 tps mustard powder
Salt and pepper

Filling:
225g / 8oz fresh spinach leaves
275g / 10oz cream cheese
2 tbs natural yoghurt
Whole nutmeg

- Pre-heat the oven to 200°C/Gas 6
- Line a swiss roll tin with greaseproof paper
- Beat the egg yolks, then stir in the cheddar cheese, cottage cheese, mustard, salt and pepper
- Whisk the egg whites until just stiff
- Fold the whites into the cheese mixture
- Spread the mixture onto the baking sheet with a palette knife, making sure you get to the edges of the tin
- Bake for 20-25 minutes, until risen and golden

Make the filling:
- Steam the spinach until just wilted, then chop finely
- In a bowl combine the spinach, cream cheese, yoghurt and enough grated nutmeg to taste
- Season with salt and pepper if needed

- Take the roulade out of the oven and flip onto another sheet of greaseproof paper
- Carefully peel off the greaseproof paper
- Spread the filling onto the roulade, but not quite to the edge
- Start rolling the roulade from the narrow edge, using the greasproof paper to help
- Slice with a sharp knife and serve with salad

QUICHE   *Serves 4*

225g / 8oz spelt flour
100g / 4oz butter or margarine
1 tsp baking powder
2 - 3 tbs cold water
3 eggs whisked
275ml / $^1/_2$ pt milk (goat, cow or soya)
1 onion finely chopped
1 tbs olive oil
1 small head of broccoli, cut into florets
1 carrot grated
100g / 4oz grated cheese
1 tsp mustard
Salt and pepper

- Pre heat oven to 190°C / Gas 5
- Steam the broccoli for a few minutes just to soften, take out and leave to one side to cool
- Make the pastry by combining the flour with the baking powder, then rub in the butter or margarine to resemble fine breadcrumbs. Sprinkle 2tbs of water over the flour and mix, keep mixing until it becomes a dough adding more water if needed
- Roll out the pastry on a floured surface and line a 19cm / 7$^1/_2$ " flan tin
- Saute the onion in the olive oil until just soft
- Place the onion, carrot, broccoli and cheese onto the pastry base
- In a jug whisk the milk, eggs, mustard, salt and pepper, pour over the pastry base
- Bake in the oven for 40 - 45 minutes until set and golden

Variation:
- **You can make the quiche without the pastry base**
- **You can make a lentil base by cooking red lentils with some bouillon until all the liquid has been absorbed. Allow to cool. When cold, press into the flan dish, (not too thick), bake in the oven for about 5 minutes. Fill the case as above**
- **Vary the fillings with different vegetables**
- **Add cooked fish instead of cheese**
- **Add cooked diced meat**

Grains

GRAINS

The best grains to use are whole, unrefined grains. When in the whole state they are rich in nutrients and gentle acting fibre.

Whole grains are also good because they are:
- Slow releasing carbohydrates
- Good for bowel problems
- Cleansing to the body
- Rich in nutrients and fibre

Try and eat whole grains most days as they help prevent cravings and low sugar troughs. Put another way, with these in your diet on a regular basis you won't feel hungry or crave. They can also help to lower cholesterol.

The grains that are best are: • Brown Rice • Millet • Quinoa
These are the ones I am focusing on in the next few pages

They are great hot or cold and can be used anywhere you would use potatoes or pasta, or just with vegetables.

Wild and red rice can be added to brown rice to add texture and colour.

BROWN RICE

Depending on how much you can eat and what you are having with the rice, will depend on how much to cook, but an average amount is 50-100g/2-4oz uncooked rice, per person.

To cook:

- **Rinse the rice in a sieve**
- **Place the rice in a saucepan, cover with plenty of water, about 4 x water to grain**
- **For flavour you can add bouillon or stock cube, but rice has got a nice flavour without this**
- **Bring to the boil then turn down the heat and simmer for about 30-40 minutes until rice is tender**
- **Turn off the heat and let the rice sit in the hot water for about 10 minutes, there shouldn't be much water left in the pan, the aim is to get the rice to absorb all the water, by doing this you are getting maximum nutrients**

Rice is lovely hot or cold
Cook extra, cool quickly by putting under cold running water, drain and place covered in the fridge. This can be used as a rice salad the next day for lunch, added to a stir fry, or used to thicken homemade soups.
Do not keep rice for more than two days when refrigerated.

TIP:
If you over cook millet it will go stodgy, so slightly undercook and leave to stand.

MILLET

Millet is a very gentle, alkaline forming food.
This grain is very easy to digest.
It has all eight essential amino acids, therefore a good protein.

To cook:

50 - 100g / 2 - 4oz millet per person
Water (about three times as much as the grain)
Bouillon or stock cube

• Put the millet, water and bouillon or stock cube into a saucepan
• Bring to the boil, then reduce the heat and simmer
  for about 15-20 minutes until tender
• Leave the millet to stand for about 10 minutes,
  it should absorb all the water

Millet doesn't have much flavour, so you can add stock
as above when cooking or you can add herbs, or spices
to the cooking water,
alternatively, Jt's French dressing (see page 76) is lovely added
at the end or when cold.
Millet is also great for stuffing vegetables.

QUINOA

This is pronounced 'Keenwa'.
It is a very old grain, around in the Egyptian times apparently.
It is high in calcium and protein.
Very good addition to a healthy diet.

To cook:

50 / 100g / 2 - 4oz per person
water 3 x the amount to quinoa
bouillon, stock cube, herbs or spices to flavour

• Wash the quinoa thoroughly in a sieve
• Put the water, quinoa and bouillon or herbs in a saucepan
• Bring to the boil then reduce the heat and simmer
  for about 20 minutes until almost cooked
• Turn off the heat and allow the quinoa to absorb the water
  for about 10 minutes

QUICK RISOTTO *Serves approximately 4*

This recipe is with chick peas but can be made with prawns, cooked chicken, or cooked fish.

This recipe makes enough for about four people or can be used for two people as a main dish and lunch the next day.

4 tbs olive oil
175g / 6oz brown rice
1 onion chopped
1 red and yellow pepper chopped
Baby sweet corn (as many as you like)
Peas or mange tout cut into two (as many as you like)
225g / 8oz mushrooms sliced
1 medium courgette diced
570 ml / 1pt vegetable stock
2 cloves garlic crushed
425g / 15oz chick peas, cooked

- Put half the oil into a deep frying pan or saucepan, sauté the onion, peppers, corn, peas or mange tout, mushrooms, courgettes and garlic until just soft
- Take out of the pan and put to one side
- Put the rest of the olive oil into the pan, add the rice, stirring to coat
- Add the stock, bring to the boil then reduce the heat and simmer until cooked (about 40 minutes)
- When all the water has been absorbed, add the sautéed vegetables and chick peas
- Heat thoroughly, stirring all the time
- Season to taste and serve with tomato salad or green salad

This is the version I would use normally, for a more elaborate risotto for a special occasion I would use risotto rice with Martini or wine, see next recipe.

TIP:
You can use rice, millet or quinoa for this recipe. Wild or red rice look nice with the brown rice as a variation.

TIP:
The base of
the risotto is the
same but you
can change the
mushrooms to
vegetables of
your choice,
just sauté first in
olive oil until
just tender as
above.
You can add
prawns, chicken
or fish as
variations.

TRADITIONAL RISOTTO   *Serves 2-4*

175g / 6oz risotto rice
Small glass martini or white wine
570 ml / 1pt vegetable stock
450g / 1lb mushrooms various, try and include Shitaki
1 large onion finely chopped
2 cloves garlic crushed
Olive oil

- Heat the stock in a small saucepan, keeping hot throughout
  on a low heat
- In a large deep frying pan, sauté the mushrooms and garlic
  in olive oil until soft
- Take out and put aside
- Put the rice into the frying pan and stir to mix in the oil
  and heat through slightly
- Pour over the martini or wine carefully, cook for a few minutes
- Then add the hot stock a little at a time, you want the stock
  to be absorbed before adding more, (about a ladle spoon,
  each time,) until the rice is cooked, (about 15-20 minutes)
- When ready add the garlic mushrooms and heat through
- Add salt and pepper to taste
- Serve with green salad, watercress, rocket etc and
  a tomato salad or steamed vegetables

EGG FRIED RICE   *Serves 2-4*

Very easy, cheap meal, to have with stir fried vegetables or salad.
Again portions vary as to how many you are cooking for.

200g / 7oz brown rice
Three times water to grain
3 eggs
Salt and pepper

- Put rice and water into a saucepan, bring to the boil,
  then turn down the heat and simmer until the rice is cooked,
  (about 40 minutes)
- Then leave the rice to stand for about 10 minutes
  to absorb all the water
- Break the eggs into a bowl
- Transfer the rice into a deep frying pan and turn the heat on
- Mix the eggs into the rice stirring gently all the time,
  trying to leave strands of egg through the rice
- Continue stirring until the egg is cooked
- Add salt and pepper to taste

PESTO RICE   *Serves 2-4*

This can be made with homemade pesto, see page 78 or a jar of pesto..

225g / 8oz brown rice
Water
Pesto sauce

- Put the rice into a saucepan and cover with water
- Bring to the boil, reduce the heat and cook the rice,
  (about 40 minutes)
- Leave to rest for 10 minutes to absorb all the water
- Mix enough pesto sauce to coat the rice
- Serve with a green salad and a tomato salad

Variation:
- **Roast some pine nuts in a dry frying pan until golden**
  brown, then sprinkle on top of the pesto rice
- **You can use pasta or potatoes instead of rice**
- **This is very nice cold the next day**

ROASTED VEGETABLES WITH QUINOA

Serves 3-4

Nice quick meal, good protein. Vary the vegetables as to availability.

200g / 7oz quinoa
1 tsp bouillon powder
1 parsnip cut into chunks
2 onions cut into large chunks
2 carrots cut into chunks
1 beetroot cut into chunks
2 sweet potatoes or squash cut into chunks
3 whole unpeeled garlic cloves
Olive oil

- Put the oven on 200°C/Gas 7
- Put all the vegetables and the garlic cloves onto a baking tray and drizzle with olive oil
- Bake in the oven
- While the vegetables are cooking, cook the quinoa
- Put the quinoa with three times the amount of water and the bouillon into a saucepan, simmer until cooked, leaving to rest for 10 minutes to absorb all the water
- When the vegetables are cooked remove from the oven
- Squeeze the garlic out of the clove and mix into the vegetables
- Put some quinoa onto a plate and pile the vegetables on top

TIP:
To reduce cooking time, cut the vegetables into smaller chunks.
• You can do extra vegetables to take for lunch with a salad or rice the next day.

Sauces

SAUCES

- Sauces make a meal.

- You can change a meal completely by adding a sauce.

In the next few pages I have given you some basic recipes;
they can be used as a base, adding different vegetables, with either fish, meat, lentils or beans or can compliment a fish or meat meal.

The sauce recipes aren't elaborate – they are quick and simple to use daily.

BASIC WHITE SAUCE

This sauce can be made from cow's milk, goat's milk or Soya milk

275ml / ½ pt milk,
25g / 1oz flour (rice flour, spelt flour or corn flour)
Salt and pepper or some boullion
15 - 25g / ½ - 1oz butter (optional)

- Mix the flour with the salt and pepper in a basin, stir some of the milk into the flour, mixing with a spoon until you have a smooth, loose paste
- Heat the milk in a saucepan until just coming to the boil, turn the heat down and gradually add the paste little at a time, stirring all the time
- Stir until the mixture comes back to a boil, then turn down the heat and cook for about 3 minutes, stirring to prevent the mixture from burning at the bottom
- Add butter (if used) and stir well

TIP:
If the sauce become lumpy, run it through a sieve, getting as much through as possible with a spoon, then put back onto heat. If the mixture is too runny just add some more flour mixed to a loose paste and heat through.

Variations on my White Sauce recipe

CHEESE SAUCE

Mix a teaspoon of English mustard to the flour, then add about 75 - 175g/3 -6oz of grated cheese after the sauce has thickened. You can use cow's cheese, hard goat's cheese or buffalo cheese.

MUSHROOM SAUCE

Cook 50g/2oz chopped mushrooms in the milk.
Take out the mushrooms; use the milk to make the white sauce as above. Add the cooked mushrooms at the end and reheat.

PARSLEY SAUCE

Add 1 - 2 tbs chopped parsley and a little lemon juice to the sauce near the end of cooking.

ONION SAUCE

Sauté a chopped onion in a little olive oil until soft, then add the milk to the onions, heat until nearly boiling, then thicken with the flour paste, cook stirring all the time until a sauce consistency.

MUSTARD SAUCE

Mix $1/2$ - 1 tsp of mustard to the paste before adding to the milk. You can use any mustard, English, Dijon, or wholegrain.

GARLIC SAUCE

Add 1 - 2 cloves of crushed garlic to the milk at the beginning of cooking. For a change you can use roasted garlic which you can buy or make your own:
Roasted garlic: Put cloves of garlic into a baking dish and cook in the oven 190°C/Gas 5 until they are soft, about 10 -15 minutes, squeeze out the garlic into the milk.

HERB SAUCE

Mix 1 tbs of chopped fresh herbs of your choice to the white sauce.

BASIC CURRY SAUCE

1 - 2 onions chopped
1 - 2 cloves of garlic crushed
1 tsp of each: ground cumin, coriander, turmeric, garam masala
$^1/_4$ - $^1/_2$ tsp chilli powder, depending on how hot you like it
1 x 400g / 14oz tinned chopped tomatoes
1 tbs tomato puree
1 tbs olive oil
vegetable stock (if required)
salt and pepper

- Put the olive oil into a frying pan, sauté the onions and spices until the onions are soft, add the tomatoes, tomato puree, salt and pepper to taste. Add vegetable stock or more tomatoes if necessary
- Cook for a few minutes
- You can add to this curry sauce: chopped apple, sultanas and/or coconut

- Add the food to be curried, meat, fish, hard boiled eggs, cooked beans, or lentils

- If using cooked meat, raw vegetables or fish, cook in the sauce for about 25-30 minutes

- For shellfish or cooked fish: add to the completed sauce and heat for 5 minutes

- Raw meat must be simmered in the sauce until cooked through, adding extra liquid if needed

- This sauce can be made with coconut milk, or stock base (use water and bouillon), instead of tomatoes

- The sauce can be thickened at the end of the cooking, with flour, mixing to a paste with water before adding

GRAVY

275ml / ¹/₂ pt water or water from the vegetables
1 tsp vegetable bouillon or stock cube
1 tbs corn flour or rice flour
Herbs of your choice (optional)

- Heat the water & bouillon or stock cube in a saucepan
- Mix the corn flour or rice flour with a little water to a loose paste
- Stir the flour mixture into the stock, stirring all the time until the gravy thickens
- Taste for flavour adding more bouillon or herbs as needed

The juice from cooked meat can be added for extra flavour, as can a little red wine or port before thickening.

GRAVY NO 2

This takes a little longer but is a really tasty gravy

25g / 1oz margarine or butter
25g / 1oz spelt, rice or corn flour
1 tsp marmite
275ml / ¹/₂ pt water or stock
¹/₂ - 1 tsp curry powder
¹/₂ -1 tsp celery seeds or mixed herbs

- Melt the margarine or butter in a saucepan, stir in the flour and curry powder, cook for a few minutes, stirring all the time
- Gradually add the water or stock stirring all the time, you might want to take the saucepan off the heat for this
- When all the water or stock is added, return to the heat
- Add the marmite, celery seeds or herbs
- Cook until thickened

CRANBERRY SAUCE

This is lovely with meat, nut, lentil or bean meals

Fresh or frozen cranberries
Sugar
Port (optional)

- Put the cranberries into a saucepan on a very low heat to extract the juice from the berries
- Be careful not to burn the bottom of the pan
- Heat until the cranberries are soft and mushy
- Add enough sugar just to take the tart taste away
- For a special occasion add some port

TIP:
This can be frozen in handy portions.
When cranberries are in season make the most of them, freeze them for use later in the season.

SWEET AND SOUR SAUCE

This sauce is lovely with vegetables, lentils, beans or meat based meals, served with brown rice.

2 tbs organic tomato ketchup
1 tbs soy sauce
1 tb cider vinegar
4 tsp corn flour
1 - 2 tsp runny honey
275ml / 1/2 pt water

- In a saucepan, blend together the ketchup, soy sauce, cider vinegar, honey and flour
- Gradually stir in the water
- Bring to the boil, turn down the heat and cook until thickened

FRENCH DRESSINGS

Ready made dressings and bottles of hemp and linseed oils are available from Jt's direct (see suppliers' list page 116). However if you wish to make your own dressings please see the following recipes.

These dressings are not only delicious but good for you. They are rich in essential fatty acids; the lack of these are associated with ADHD (Attention deficit and hyperactivity disorder).

Beautiful skin is from the inside out, these essential oils combined with a healthy diet are great for glowing healthy skin.

Essential fatty acids are involved in virtually every bodily function, the inflammatory process, the healing & repairing process, the immune system, the neural circuits in the brain, the cardio-vascular system, the digestive and reproductive system, the body thermostat and the calorie loss mechanism.

The dressings are rich in these essential fats, which are lacking in most diets today. Use them on salads, rice, millet or quinoa, jacket potatoes, steamed or stir fried vegetables. The oil must not be heated, so add to the food at the end of cooking.

Get yourself a lovely container for your dressings. Do not store them in plastic. Use glass or china, as oils will absorb chemicals from the plastic. Make up a bottle and keep in the fridge.

Use a good olive oil, first pressed – cold pressed is the best. This means it is the first pressing of the olive and they haven't used high temperatures during the process, therefore not damaging the oil.

TIP:
You can vary the flavour by adding more or less garlic, herbs or chilli.

FRENCH DRESSING

1 bottle or jug of your choice for the dressing
275ml / $\frac{1}{2}$ pt olive oil
275ml / $\frac{1}{2}$ pt linseed oil
1 - 2 cloves of garlic crushed
Pinch black pepper
1 tsp mustard, Dijon, English or wholegrain
4tbs organic cider vinegar

- Mix altogether in a jar or bottle
- Shake really well
- Store in the fridge, shaking well before use

HEMP DRESSING

Hemp oil is high in omega 3, 6 and 9 essential fats.
Hemp dressing has a delicious delicate flavour.

1 container for dressing
275ml / 1/2 pt hemp oil
275ml / 1/2 pt olive oil
1 - 2 cloves garlic crushed
pinch black pepper
1/4 tsp mustard Dijon, English or wholegrain
4 tbs organic cider vinegar

• Mix altogether in the jar or bottle used
• Shake well
• Store in the fridge, shaking well before use

You can also make the Hemp dressing with just hemp oil,
because the oil is such a light oil it tastes delicious.

TIP:
You can vary the flavour by adding herbs or chillies, changing the amount of garlic to your taste. Experiment with the basic recipe.

TOMATO SAUCE

This makes a lovely rich sauce by adding olive oil. For a lighter sauce
use only enough olive oil to sauté the onions.

1 - 2 onions chopped
2 x 400g / 14oz tinned chopped tomatoes
2 garlic cloves crushed
2 tbs tomato puree
4 tbs olive oil
2 tbs chopped fresh herbs or 2 tsp of dried herbs, basil,
mixed herbs, oregano, or rosemary are all good in this

• Sauté the onions in a little olive oil, until soft
• Add the tomatoes, puree, garlic. If using dried herbs add
  now along with the rest of the olive oil, stir well
• Simmer for about 10-20 minutes depending on how thick
  you want the sauce, the longer you cook it, the thicker it gets
• If using fresh herbs, add about 10 minutes
  before the end of cooking

TIP:
This recipe can be made more economical by adding vegetable stock with the tomatoes, then thickening the mixture at the end with corn flour if needed.

TZATZIKI

This is good as a salad dressing, on jacket potatoes, or mixed with rice, millet, quinoa, pasta, beans or lentils.

200g / 7oz natural live yoghurt
1/2 cucumber grated
1 - 2 cloves garlic crushed
Lemon juice (optional)
Pinch cayenne pepper

- Mix altogether in a bowl
- This will keep refrigerated for 2-3 days, simply stir before using

CURRY DRESSING

Lovely mixed with rice, millet, quinoa, pasta, potatoes, beans, lentils or vegetables.

200g / 7oz natural live yoghurt
1/2 tsp of cumin, coriander, turmeric, garam masala
little salt and pepper (optional)

- Mix together in a bowl
- It will keep refrigerated for 2-3 days, stirring before use

PESTO SAUCE

15g / 1/2 oz fresh basil leaves
120g / 41/2 oz pine kernels
2 garlic cloves crushed
6 tbs olive oil
50g / 2oz freshly grated Parmesan
Salt and pepper

- Remove the basil leaves from the stalks
- In a food processor put the basil leaves, pine nuts, garlic, olive oil and Parmesan cheese
- Blend until a smooth paste
- Add salt and pepper if needed

MAYONNAISE

Once you've made your own you won't want to go back to bought ones!

2 egg yolks
Good pinch salt and pepper
Good pinch mustard powder
275ml / ½ pt olive oil
2 dessertspoons organic cider vinegar

- In a food processor put the egg yolks, salt, pepper and mustard powder and blend
- With the processor still on, gradually add all of the olive oil, drops at a time
- Gradually the mixture will become thicker
- Turn off the processor and stir in the cider vinegar
- Put into a glass or china container and store in the fridge
- Use within three days

Variations:
- Add crushed garlic with the vinegar
- Add 1tbs chopped parsley,
     1-2 tbs chopped gherkins
     1-2 tbs chopped capers
- Chopped herbs of your choice, coriander, basil, dill are nice

Vegetables

VEGETABLES

Local, seasonal vegetables, preferably organic or grown without sprays are essential for nutrient value and flavour.

There are a variety of good organic vegetable box schemes available, (see suppliers list). These boxes are great, they are straight from the farm into the box and straight to your door. Plus they haven't travelled half way across the world! They are not as expensive as you think and compare well with supermarkets, but they are seasonal, so with most box schemes you can't pick and choose, you have what is in season. Don't let this put you off, as I have found this was a good way of getting to use vegetables I might not have normally used, and I have to say I found I loved.

If you only want enough vegetables for one person, most places do various sized boxes to suit most households, so make some enquiries.

There are also farmers markets.
They sell lovely local, organic produce, that will easily last a week or two in the fridge. Check out where the nearest one is to you, by going onto the farmers markets web site (see under the section, suppliers list)

Don't miss out on the wonderful flavours of locally grown produce.
We are meant to eat seasonally grown vegetables and salads.

With some of the vegetable recipes below, I haven't put how many they will serve, you can use as many or as few as you wish, depending on how many people you are cooking for.

ROASTED VEGETABLES WITH NUTS
Serves 4

2 red peppers cut into 2.5cm / 1" squares
2 yellow peppers cut into 2.5cm / 1" squares
2 red onions cut into chunks
1 fennel bulb sliced (optional)
16 baby tomatoes
8 whole garlic cloves
225g / 8oz cashew nuts
Olive oil

- Pre heat the oven to 190C / gas 5
- Put the vegetables, nuts and garlic into a baking dish
- Drizzle with olive oil
- Bake in the oven for about 30 minutes until the vegetables are soft and juicy
- Squeeze out the garlic from the cloves onto the vegetables
- Serve with fresh pasta, rice or quinoa

SAUTED CARROT AND PARSNIPS   *Serves 2-3*

This is lovely with fish or meat.

2 carrots grated
1 parsnip grated
1tbs olive oil
1-2 cloves garlic, crushed
Lemon juice to taste

- Heat the oil in a large frying pan
- Sauté the carrots, parsnips and garlic in the oil until just soft
- Add lemon juice to taste
- Serve hot.

ROASTED TOMATOES

These are nice served with fish, meat or vegetarian dishes,
well anything really!

Baby tomatoes
   (if tomatoes are larger then cut into half or quarters)
Olive oil
Whole unpeeled garlic cloves, about 6, or more if wished
Rosemary sprigs

* Pre-heat the oven to 200°C/Gas 6
* Place the tomatoes, whole garlic cloves, and rosemary sprigs
  into a baking dish
* Drizzle with a little olive oil
* Bake in the oven, until the tomatoes are soft,
  (about 30-40 minutes)
* Take the dish out of the oven, and squeeze the garlic out of
  the cloves (being careful not to burn yourself)

TIP:
You could add goat's cheese or Hallumi cheese to the tomatoes and garlic before cooking.
You could add fresh basil leaves near the end of cooking, instead of rosemary.

SPINACH AND NUTMEG   *Serves 2-4*

Particularly good with fish, pasta or rice.

Spinach
Whole nutmeg
Créme fraiche or natural yoghurt

* Very lightly steam the spinach, until just wilted
* Remove the spinach from the steamer, and cut into shreds
  with a knife
* Place the spinach into a frying pan with some créme fraiche
  or natural live yoghurt, and some grated nutmeg to taste.
* Heat through gently

TIP:
Instead of the cheese, you could use a whole anchovy in each pepper. (These can be bought in a tin from most supermarkets). This is a tasty variation.

ROASTED RED AND YELLOW PEPPERS

Serves 2-4

1 yellow pepper
1 red pepper
4 cloves whole unpeeled garlic
100g / 4oz goat's cheese or Haloumi cheese, cut into four pieces
8 baby tomatoes
Rosemary sprigs (optional)
Olive oil

- Pre-heat the oven to 200°C / Gas 6
- Cut the peppers in half, and scoop out the seeds, rinse under the tap
- Place the peppers into a baking dish, (cavity facing up)
- In each pepper place, two baby tomatoes, a piece of cheese, whole garlic clove and sprig of rosemary (if used).
- Drizzle a little olive oil over the peppers
- Bake in the oven until the peppers are soft, (about 30 minutes)

ROASTED MEDITERRANIAN VEGETABLES

Use as many vegetables as required.

Red peppers cut in half and de-seeded then cut into quarters
Yellow peppers cut in half and de-seeded then cut into quarters
Whole, unpeeled garlic cloves
Tomatoes cut into halves or quarters
Aubergine sliced (cut into half or quarters if large)
Red onions cut into halves or quarters
Olive oil
Basil leaves

- Pre-heat the oven to 200°C / Gas 6
- Place all the vegetables and garlic cloves onto a baking sheet
- Drizzle with olive oil
- Give the tray a little shake so all the vegetables are lightly coated
- Bake in the oven until the vegetables are just cooked (about 30-40 minutes)
- Add the basil leaves at the end of cooking
- Take the tray out of the oven, squeeze the garlic out of the cloves onto the vegetables, and serve

ROASTED ROOT VEGETABLES

The amount of vegetables used, depends on how many you are cooking for. You can use all or any combination of the vegetables in this recipe.

Sweet potatoes
Parsnips
Onions
Beetroot
Squash or pumpkin
Carrots
Fennel
Celeriac
Garlic cloves crushed
Olive oil

- Pre-heat the oven to 200°C/Gas 6
- Cut all the vegetables into chunks (the larger the chunks, the longer the cooking time)
- Put the vegetables into a deep baking dish, mix in the crushed garlic, and drizzle with olive oil
- Toss the vegetables to coat.
- Bake in the oven, (taking the vegetables out of the oven during the cooking time, to shake, so they cook evenly), until the vegetables are just tender (about 30-40 minutes)

TIP:
Cook extra to have cold in a salad or omelette the next day

RATATOUILLE   *Serves 4*

2 medium sized aubergines chopped into cubes
4 courgettes sliced
2 onions chopped
2 cloves garlic crushed
1 large red pepper chopped
1 large yellow pepper chopped
225g / 8oz tomatoes chopped
1 tbs tomato puree
6 tbs olive oil
Fresh basil leaves
Salt and pepper

- Sauté the onions in the olive oil for a few minutes
- Add all the other vegetables and tomato puree to the onions
- Cover and cook gently, until the vegetables are soft, but not mushy, (about 30-35 minutes)
- Tear the basil leaves and add to the ratatouille
- Add salt and pepper to taste
- This can be served hot or cold

SAUTED GRATED VEGETABLES

This is great with any dish. The vegetables are nice and moist.

Carrots
Parsnips
Celeriac
Olive oil
Fresh ginger
Garlic cloves crushed
Chopped parsley (optional)

- Grate all the vegetables
- Heat the oil in a deep frying pan, add the grated vegetables, garlic, and grated ginger to taste
- Cook, stirring a few times, until the vegetables are just soft
- Serve hot, with chopped parsley if wished

VARIATION ON CARROTS

Carrots grated
Garlic cloves crushed
Juice of orange
Olive oil

- Grate the carrots
- Sauté the carrots and garlic in the olive oil, until just soft
- Add fresh orange juice to taste

ROASTED FENNEL

I never knew what to do with fennel; this is a quick and tasty way to use them. Great with other vegetables or cold in salad.

Fennel sliced
Olive oil

- Pre-heat oven to 200°C/Gas 6
- Put the fennel and olive oil into a baking sheet, and shake to coat with oil
- Bake in the oven until soft, (about 20 minutes)

CELERIAC AND POTATO MASH   *Serves 4-6*

350g / 12oz potatoes
350g / 12oz celeriac
Little butter or margarine
Salt and pepper to taste

- Cut off the outside of the celeriac, and chop into chunks
- Cut the potatoes into chunks
- Steam the celeriac and potatoes until soft
- Put the cooked vegetables into a saucepan and mash, adding a little butter or margarine
- If the vegetables are too dry, add a little milk
- Add salt and pepper to taste
- Serve hot with any meal

PARSNIP OR SWEET POTATO CHIPS

Parsnips or sweet potatoes
Olive oil
Salt

- Pre-heat the oven to 200°C/Gas 6
- Cut the parsnips or sweet potatoes into thin chips
- Put them into a bowl, drizzle with olive oil, stir to coat
- With a slotted spoon, take the vegetables out of the oil, and place onto a baking sheet
- Sprinkle with salt
- Bake in the oven until crispy

POTATO CHIPS

TIP:
For speed, partially steam the potatoes first before cutting into chips

Potatoes
Olive oil
Salt

- Pre heat the oven to 220°C/Gas 7
- Cut the potatoes into chips
- Place the chips into a bowl, and drizzle with olive oil, stir to coat
- Take the chips out with a slotted spoon, and place onto a baking sheet
- Sprinkle on some salt
- Bake in the oven until crispy

Variation:
- **Add spices to the oil, before coating the potatoes, for example: cumin, coriander, garan masala, turmeric, chilli.**
- **The potatoes could be cut into wedges instead of chips.**

COLESLAW   *Serves 4-6*

$^1/_2$ **white cabbage shredded**
2 carrots grated
1 - 2 onions finely chopped
Homemade or organic jar mayonnaise
Natural live yoghurt

- Put the cabbage, carrot and onion into a large bowl
- Mix enough mayonnaise with natural yoghurt,
  (half and half), to coat the vegetables
- Store in a covered bowl in the fridge
- This will keep for a couple of days in the fridge.
- Stir before use

WINTER COLESLAW   *Serves 4-6*

450g / 1lb sprouts
2 - 3 carrots grated
Bunch spring onions chopped
Homemade mayonnaise or organic jar mayonnaise
Natural live yoghurt

- Cut the bottom off the sprouts, and remove any
  damaged outer leaves, (leaving as much as possible)
- In a food processor, slice the sprouts thinly (they won't grate)
- Mix the sprouts, carrots and spring onions together
  in a large bowl
- Combine enough mayonnaise with yoghurt (half and half),
  to coat the vegetables
- Store in a covered bowl in the fridge
- This will last for a couple of days in the fridge,
  stir before use

Variation:
- **Fruity coleslaw: Add diced apple, orange segments and/or**
  dried fruit to the finished recipe
- **Add walnuts, pine nuts or almonds**
- **Add sunflower or pumpkin seeds**

Salads

SALADS

- **Salads are one of the most important foods in the diet. Eating fresh, raw vegetables and fruit is the best way to obtain all the essential vitamins and minerals.**
- **Salads are not boring. Vary salads by adding fruits, salad and vegetables together. The combination is almost endless. I have given you a few suggestions, but be imaginative.**
- **Salads aren't just a summer dish, salad leaves are available all year round from some farmers markets, farm shops and local shops.**
- **Or if you are really keen grow your own, rocket grows like wild fire apparently, or land cress (like watercress that can be grown in pots) and other dark salad leaves. Try winter vegetables, for example, beetroot, cauliflower and mushrooms.**

SPROUTING

When a bean or lentil is sprouted it becomes an amazing food, full of nutrients, for example, B vitamins, Vitamin C, iron, zinc and many more. They can be used on salads, or put into hot dishes at the end, (to maintain nutrient value), for example in a stir fry, curry or soup. Therefore they can be used all year. You will need a sprouter. This can be purchased from good health food shops. They vary in shape and price.

THREE DAY SPROUT MIX

(from health food shops or Jt's – see suppliers' list)

Sprouter
Water
1/2 - 1 cup of sprout mix
Deep bowl

- Put the sprout mix into the bowl, and cover with water.
  Leave to soak for about 8 hours or overnight
- Drain and rinse
- Put evenly onto the sprouter trays
- Water twice a day
- In three days they will have sprouted
- Remove the sprouts from the tray and store in a container in the fridge
- The whole of the **sprouted** bean is edible
- Have daily if possible. Use within three to four days

SIX DAY SPROUT MIX
• Sprinkle lightly onto the sprouter tray
• Water twice a day
• In six days it will have grown to look like cress
• Take it all off the tray, and store in an open container in the fridge
• Use within three to four days

EXAMPLES OF SALADS
Don't be afraid to use various combinations, using seasonal vegetables and salad. Vary the dressings, see the section on sauces for ideas.

• **Grated raw beetroot and grated apple**
• **Grated raw beetroot and grated carrot**
  (lovely with French dressing, page 76)
• **Radish, red onion, shredded red cabbage**
• **Apple, celery and walnut**
• **Coleslaw**
• **Green leaves with hot or cold roasted vegetables**
• **Raw sliced mushrooms, spring onions, bean sprouts and avocado pear**
• **Red and yellow peppers, halumi cheese, watercress**
• **Watercress, fennel bulb sliced thinly, radish**
• **Grated raw celeriac, combine with natural yoghurt, mayonnaise and a little mustard**

• Vary flavour by adding either olives, sun dried tomatoes, herbs, dressings or pesto
• Vary look and texture by chopping, grating, or slicing, the vegetables. You can do this by hand or using a food processor
• Roasted vegetables are lovely on salads
• Use either diced apple, grapes, slices of orange, fresh pineapple, banana, pear or kiwi to salads
• Use dried fruit, raisins, apricots, etc
• Salads can be made with brown rice, millet, quinoa, pasta, rice noodles, or bean sprouts
• Add cooked beans and lentils
• Add sprouted beans and lentils
• Add protein, egg, fish or meat

The following examples are great on their own, combined or used in combination with the above protein, grain or in a pancake wrap.

AVOCADO AND NUT SALAD   *Serves 1-2*

1 avocado pear
1 bunch of watercress chopped
50g - 100g / 2 - 4oz pine nuts
Juice of $^1/_2$ lemon

- Cut the avocado in half, take out the stone and
  with a spoon take out the flesh.
- Put the avocado in a bowl, drizzle the lemon juice on top,
  gently combine, (this prevents the avocado going brown)
- Add the watercress and pine nuts

BEANS WITH SALSA SALAD   *Serves 2-4*

225g / 8oz red kidney beans (or beans of your choice)
$^1/_2$ - $^1/_4$ cucumber diced
1 red pepper diced
100g / 4oz sweet corn

Salsa:
1 x 400g / 14oz tinned chopped tomatoes
1 onion finely chopped
1 clove garlic crushed
$^1/_2$ - 1 tsp chilli powder
1 dst olive oil
Salt and pepper

To make the salsa:
- Sauté the onion and chilli powder in the olive oil
  until the onions are soft
- Add the garlic, tomatoes, salt and pepper to taste
- Cook until the mixture becomes thick
- Test for flavour
- Add the red kidney beans, cucumber, red pepper and corn
- Nice hot or cold

MIXED PEPPER SALAD   *Serves 2*

1 red pepper sliced
1 yellow pepper sliced
50 - 100g / 2 - 4oz sunflower seeds
2 sticks celery sliced
1 apple diced

- Toast the sunflower seeds by placing in a dry frying pan, heat until the seeds turn golden brown
- Put the peppers, celery and apple into a bowl, sprinkle on the sunflower seeds

SPROUTED SALAD   *Serves 2*

2 handfuls of three day sprout mix (see page 91)
50 - 100g / 2 - 4oz coleslaw (page 89)
50g / 2oz walnuts
1 apple diced

- Put the coleslaw into a dish or container, mix in the diced apple, top with the sprout mix and walnuts

HERB AND YOGHURT SALAD   *Serves 2/4*

2 carrots grated
$1/2$ cucumber diced
50 - 75g / 2 - 3oz celeriac grated or celery chopped
225g / 8oz natural yoghurt
1 clove garlic crushed
Juice of $1/2$ lemon
1 tbs coriander or mint chopped

- Mix together the yoghurt, garlic, lemon juice, coriander or mint
- In a bowl place the carrots, cucumber and celeriac, top with some yoghurt dressing

CURRIED RICE   *Serves 2-4*

100g / 4oz cooked brown rice
1 apple diced
100g / 4oz red kidney beans or bean of your choice
4 tomatoes chopped or whole baby tomatoes
50g / 2oz dessicated coconut
3 tbs natural yoghurt
1 tbs organic mayonnaise
1 tsp organic curry paste (available from health food shops)

- In a bowl mix together the yoghurt, mayonnaise and curry paste
- Add the rest of the ingredients to the curry sauce, stir to combine

TIP:
The sauce will keep in the fridge for three days

GREEN LEAF SALAD   *Serves 1-2*

As much green leaves as you would like:
  rocket, baby spinach leaves, watercress etc
50g / 4oz bamboo shoots
1 sweet potato diced or ¼ squash diced
Drizzle olive oil
French dressing (page 76)

- Place the sweet potato or squash into a baking dish and drizzle with olive oil. Bake in the oven until it is just soft
- Take out and allow to cool
- Put the leaves and bamboo shoots into a bowl or container, mix in the sweet potato
- Drizzle with French dressing

MARINADED PEPPER SALAD   *Serves 4-6*

1 clove garlic crushed
6 tbs olive oil
3 tbs cider vinegar
$1/2$ tsp ground coriander or 1 tbs fresh coriander chopped
1 tsp sugar or honey
salt
1 red pepper sliced into thin strips
1 yellow pepper sliced into thin strips
1 green pepper sliced into thin strips

- Mix the garlic, oil, vinegar, coriander and sugar or honey to a paste
- Put the sliced peppers into a bowl, add the paste and stir until the peppers are coated
- Cover the bowl and keep in the fridge
- Use in salads or rice dishes

FRUITS AND SALAD   *Serves 1-2*

1 apple diced or grated
1 orange peeled and cut into chunks
2 sticks celery diced
50g / 4oz walnuts

- Combine all the ingredients together, nice with green leaves

RICE AND APRICOT SALAD   *Serves 2*

50 - 100g / 2 - 4oz cooked brown rice
50g / 4oz dried apricots chopped
50g / 4oz almonds
French dressing (page 76) or lemon juice, salt and pepper

- Pre heat the oven to 200°C / Gas 6
- Place the almonds onto a baking sheet and bake for about 10 minutes, take out of the oven and cool
- Roughly chop the almonds
- In a bowl mix the rice, apricots and almonds
- Either drizzle with the French dressing or lemon juice, salt and pepper, give a good stir

BEETROOT SALAD   *Serves 2-4*

1 raw beetroot grated
$1/2$ carrot grated
Dark salad leaves
French dressing (page 76)

- Place the salad leaves into a dish, place some beetroot and carrot on top
- Drizzle with dressing

Variations:
- Grated beetroot with grated apple
- Grated beetroot and diced orange segments

GRAPE AND CHEESE SALAD   *Serves 1-2*

100 - 175g / 4 - 6oz organic grapes with seeds (more nutritious)
100g / 4oz goats cheese diced
$1/4$ cucumber diced
2 tomatoes chopped
50g / 2oz dates stoned and chopped or banana sliced (mix with lemon juice to prevent it going brown)

- Combine all the ingredients together

OLIVE AND FENNEL SALAD   *Serves 2*

2 handfuls three day sprouted mix (see page 91)
1 red pepper sliced
1 small head fennel sliced
8 olives
French dressing (see page 76)

- In a bowl mix together the sprout mix, pepper, fennel and olives
- Drizzle over the French dressing and stir

SALAD WITH PINEAPPLE   *Serves 2*

2 thick slices of fresh pineapple cut into chunks
2-4 sticks celery diced
1 red pepper sliced
25g/1oz shredded coconut

- Mix all the ingredients together

BANANA AND NUT SALAD   *Serves 2*

I love the combination of the sweet banana with the sharp watercress.

1 banana sliced
1 bunch watercress roughly chopped
50 - 100g / 2 - 4oz walnuts
Juice of $1/2$ lemon

- Toss the banana in the lemon juice (to prevent it going brown)
- Place the watercress onto a plate or container, top with the banana, walnuts and celery
- Drizzle with French dressing if wished

AVOCADO AND BROCCOLI SALAD   *Serves 1-2*

1 avocado pear, stoned
1 head of broccoli cut into small florets
25g / 1oz sun dried tomatoes
50g / 2oz organic peanuts
Juice of $1/2$ lemon
French dressing or yoghurt with herbs

- Scoop out the flesh from the avocado and toss in the lemon juice (to prevent going brown)
- Place the avocado, broccoli, sun dried tomatoes and peanuts into a bowl
- Drizzle French dressing over the top and gently stir to combine OR mix chopped fresh herbs (coriander, mint or basil) with natural live yoghurt, place a spoonful on top of the salad

GREEK SALAD   *Serves 2*

4 tomatoes cut into quarters
6 olives
1 red onion sliced
$1/4$ cucumber diced
$1/2$ block of Feta cheese diced
1 dst olive oil
$1/2$ juice lemon
Few basil leaves torn (optional)

- Put the tomatoes, olives, onion, cucumber and Feta into a bowl
- Drizzle with olive oil and lemon juice
- Gently combine, adding the basil leaves if used

PESTO SALAD   *Serves 2-3*

100g / 4oz cooked rice or pasta
3 - 4 tomatoes diced
2 sticks celery chopped
100g / 4oz cooked green beans
100g / 4oz mushrooms sliced
Pesto (page 78)

- Mix all the ingredients together except the pesto
- Add just enough pesto to coat the rice

Miscellaneous

MISCELLANEOUS

BREAD

This recipe is so easy and makes lovely bread.
Spelt flour is the old wheat grain. It was around in the Roman times, which means that some people can tolerate spelt flour when they can't tolerate normal wheat. Spelt flour can be used to make things exactly like normal wheat.

450g / 1 lb 2oz spelt flour
500ml pot of natural live yoghurt
2 tsp bicarbonate

- Pre-heat oven to 220°C/Gas 7
- In a bowl, mix the bicarbonate with the flour
- Make a well in the centre of the flour and add the yoghurt, mix well, to dough like consistency
- Make into a large round shape or individual rolls and either place onto a floured baking sheet, or put dough into a greased and floured 1 lb loaf tin
- Bake in the oven on the high temperature for about 10 minutes (8 minutes for rolls), then turn the heat down to 190C/Gas 5, and bake for a further 30 minutes (15 minutes for rolls)
- If the bread isn't cooked inside, then just pop back into the oven for a few minutes more
- This bread is lovely as it is or try some of the samples below

Variations:
- **Add roasted garlic, sun dried tomatoes, olives or roasted peppers**
- **Halumi cheese or goats cheese in the centre with rosemary**
- **Grated carrot with cinnamon (sweet version)**
- **Small pieces of apple with nutmeg**
- **Sunflower and pumpkin seeds**
- **Sesame or poppy seeds**
- **Dried fruit with mixed spice**

TIP:
You can freeze the bread (slice first) and rolls. Don't overcook the rolls on the high temperature or they become too crispy – you just want to seal the outside before turning down the heat.

TIP:
Freeze any left
over garlic butter.

GARLIC BREAD

Spelt flour dough (see previous recipe)
250g / 9oz butter cut into chunks
2 cloves garlic crushed
1 tbs dried mixed herbs or oregano
Juice of $1/2$ a lemon

- Form dough into two small French sticks
- Bake in the oven 220°C/Gas 7 for 8-10 minutes, turn down the oven to 190C/Gas 5 and bake for a further 15-20 minutes
- Put the French sticks onto a cooling rack
- In a food processor put the butter, garlic, herbs, lemon juice, and blend until soft
- Cut slits into the bread, slanting them, about $1/2$ - 1 inch apart
- Spread some garlic butter onto both sides of each slit, and a little on top of the loaves
- Cover each one with foil
- Put into the oven 220°C/Gas 7 for about 10 minutes, then open the foil to bake for a further 5 minutes, to crisp the top a little
- Take out of the oven, and cut through each slit. Serve warm

PANCAKES

275ml / $1/2$ pt milk (organic cows, goats or soya)
4oz rice flour
2 eggs
Olive oil

- Put the milk, flour and eggs into a liquidizer and blend until smooth
- With a pastry brush wipe a little olive oil onto a frying pan and heat
- Add just enough batter to coat the base of the frying pan. (About 2 tbs. Turn the pan so mixture just covers the bottom.)
- Cook for 1 - 2 minutes or until the underside is cooked
- Flip the pancake over and cook for another minute
- Remove from the pan and place onto greaseproof paper
- Re-wipe the pan with more oil and continue as above, until all the mixture has been used placing greaseproof paper between each pancake
- When cool put them into a freezer bag and freeze
- When needed take the pancake/s out and defrost in the fridge or in a very low oven for a few minutes

JELLY   *Serves 4*

570ml / 1pt pure fruit juice
50g / 2oz icing sugar
1 sachet of organic or vegetarian gelatine

- Whisk the icing sugar into the juice, adding more if wished
- Heat $1/2$ cup of juice, sprinkle the gelatine onto the hot juice, stir or whisk briskly, until thoroughly mixed
- Add to the rest of the juice and whisk well (or follow the instructions on the packet)
- Put into individual dishes or one large dish
- Put into the fridge until set

TIP:
Fresh fruit can also be used, just heat gently to extract as much juice as possible. Press through a sieve. Follow the above instructions.

BROWN RICE PUDDING   *Serves 4*

100g / 4oz short grain brown rice
Milk
Natural custard powder
Honey, organic maple syrup or rice syrup

- Rinse the rice in a sieve
- Place the rice in a saucepan, cover with plenty of water, about 4 x water to grain
- Bring to the boil, reduce the heat and simmer for about 30-40 minutes, until the rice is tender
- Drain off any excess water
- Put the rice back into the saucepan, and cover with milk
- Add enough honey, maple syrup or rice syrup to taste
- Heat gently
- Mix about 1 tablespoon of the custard powder with a little milk, to a soft paste
- Add this to the rice, stirring all the time until thickened (If the mixture is too thick add more milk, if too runny add more custard powder, firstly mixed to paste as above)
- Test for sweetness

Variations:
You can add grated nutmeg, or cinnamon, or vanilla essence to the rice.

CRUMBLE   *Serves 4-6*

You can use any fruit for this crumble.

100g / 4oz rice flour or spelt flour
100g / 4oz porridge oats
100g / 4oz margarine or butter
50g / 2oz sugar or honey
Fruit of choice cooked

- Pre-heat oven to 190C / Gas 5
- Place the fruit into one larger baking dish or individual ones
- In a bowl place the flour and margarine or butter
- Rub the fat into the flour with your fingertips,
  until you have a breadcrumb consistency
- Add the oats and sugar if used, or you can drizzle honey on
  the top of the crumble after cooking
- Top the fruit with the crumble mixture and lightly press down
- Bake in the oven for about 15-20 minutes
- Serve with custard or yoghurt

CAROB TREATS

Sweet paper cases
Carob chocolate drops

- Melt the carob drops in a double boiler or in a bowl
  over hot water
- Remove the carob from the heat
- Add any of the ingredients below
- Spoon a good teaspoonful into the sweet cases and
  allow to cool
- When cool store in an airtight container

Additions:
- **Toasted hazel nuts or almonds.**
  Toast by placing on a baking sheet and bake in the oven
  (200°C / Gas 6) for 10-15 minutes, allow to cool
  before adding to the melted carob
- **Sunflower and pumpkin seeds**
- **Puffed rice (available from health food shops)**
- **Popcorn**

FLAPJACKS

350g / 12oz dried dates
4 tbs water
225g / 8oz porridge oats
150g / 5oz butter or margarine

- Pre-heat the oven to 190C / Gas 5
- Put the dates into a saucepan with the water, heat gently until the dates are soft, like a purée (adding more water if it goes dry)
- Melt the butter or margarine in a saucepan (do not let it boil)
- Put the oats into a mixing bowl, add the butter or margarine and the dates
- Mix well
- Place into a shallow baking tray
- Smooth over the surface with a palette knife
- Bake in the oven for 25-30 minutes, until set and golden brown
- Let it cool a little, then mark into portions while still warm
- Leave to cool in the tin on a wire rack
- When cold cut into portions, remove from the tin and store in an airtight container

Variations:
- **Add sunflower seeds**
- **Add chopped nuts**
- **Put half of the flapjack mixture into a shallow baking dish, top with pureed apple, dates or apricots, place the rest of the flapjack mixture on top and press down lightly, bake as above**

> TIP:
> If you are unable to eat oats you could use rice flakes.
> Break them down slightly in a food processor, before adding the melted butter or margarine, then let them stand for a few minutes to soften, before adding the pureed dates. Continue as above.

FAT AND SUGAR FREE FRUIT CAKE

165g / 5 $^1/_2$ oz spelt flour
$^1/_2$ tsp each of nutmeg and cinnamon
3 tsp baking powder
225g / 8oz mixed dried fruit
6 tbs apple juice
1 tbs runny honey
1 egg

- Pre-heat the oven to 180°C / Gas 4
- Place the flour, cinnamon, nutmeg, baking powder and
  dried fruit into a bowl, stir to combine
- In a jug put the apple juice, honey and egg, whisk to combine
- Add the juice mixture to the dry ingredients, mix together
- Put the mixture into a greased and floured 1 lb loaf tin
- Bake in the oven for 40 - 60 minutes

WHOLEMEAL SCONES WITH YOGURT

225g / 8oz spelt flour
1$^1/_2$ tsp baking powder
25g / 1oz butter or margarine
150ml / $^1/_4$ pt natural live yoghurt (room temperature)

- Pre-heat oven to 200°C / Gas 6
- In a bowl or food processor mix the flour and
  baking powder together
- Rub in the butter or margarine until it resembles
  fine breadcrumbs
- Add enough yoghurt to make the consistency of a soft dough
- Knead lightly on a floured surface
- Either form into one large circle about 7" round and score
  the dough into eight sections or roll dough out slightly
  to about 5cm/2" thick, using a pastry cutter cut into rounds
- Place onto a floured baking sheet and bake for about 15-20 mins

Variations:
Add to the breadcrumb mixture before the yoghurt
- **Dried fruit**
- **Chopped fresh apple and nutmeg**
- **Grated carrot and cinammon**
- **Grated or diced cheese**
- **Chopped fresh herbs**

TOASTED OATS

This can be used as a cereal, in yoghurt or just as a snack.
It keeps well in an airtight container.

450g / 1 lb jumbo oats
6 tbs olive oil
3 tbs honey

- Pre-heat the oven to 190°C/Gas 5
- Put the honey and oil into a saucepan, warm through gently, stir to combine
- Put the oats into a deep baking tin
- Coat the oats with the warm oil and honey, until the oats are just coated (not too moist)
- Bake in the oven, stirring now and again until all the oats are golden brown
- Take out of the oven and cool
- Store in an airtight container

Variations:
- **Use just olive oil with a tsp of vanilla extract**
- **Add cinnamon or nutmeg to the oats before cooking**
- **Add coconut, dried fruit, seeds, or nuts to the cooled, cooked oats**

POPCORN

Very cheap and easy breakfast cereal, as a snack or with yoghurt.
Do not remove the lid from the pan while the corn is popping –
it can cause a nasty burn.

Organic popping corn
1 tbs olive oil

- Heat the oil in a deep saucepan
- Add enough popcorn to generously cover the bottom of the pan
- Put a tight fitting lid on and shake the pan to coat the popcorn
- When you can hear the corn popping turn down the heat slightly
- Shake the pan now and again to prevent the corn from burning
- When you can't hear the corn popping anymore, take the pan off the heat and allow to cool
- Take off the lid carefully
- Put into a bowl to cool, when cold store in an airtight container

Variation:
- **Toast in olive oil & honey as in previous recipe**
- **Add coconut, seeds, nuts, dried fruit to popped corn**
- **Toast in olive oil with chilli or curry powder for a savoury version**

YOGURT AND APRICOT WHIP   *Serves 4-6*

450ml / 3/4 pt natural live yoghurt
250g / 9oz dried apricots
Water

- Put the dried apricots and a little water into a saucepan
- Heat gently, until the apricots are soft
  (adding a little more water if needed, cool)
- Put the apricots and yoghurt into a liquidizer,
  blend until smooth
- Put into individual bowls or one larger bowl
- Cover and keep refrigerated – it will keep for a couple of
  days in the fridge

Variations:
- **Puree different dried or fresh fruits**
- **Top with toasted flaked almonds (toast by placing the almonds into a dry frying pan and heat, stirring, until all the almonds are golden brown, take off and cool)**
- **Top with toasted sunflower seeds (toast as for flaked almonds above)**
- **For a special occasion, add double cream to the yoghurt (about 250ml / 8floz), add the fruit and blend**

PATÉS

Patés are lovely served with crackers, bread or toast.
Or to stuff vegetables for example; baby tomatoes, celery, cucumber. You can also use lettuce leaves to make into parcels, just put some paté into the centre of the leaf, fold the bottom of the leaf up, the sides of the leaf over to the centre, then the top of the leaf over them, so you have a parcel. Also a nice filling for jacket potatoes.

TUNA PATE

1 x small tin tuna drained
1 dessertspoon mayonnaise
1 dessertspoon natural yoghurt
1 tsp lime juice
1 tbs fresh chives chopped

- Put the tuna into a bowl and mash
- Add the mayonnaise, yoghurt, lime juice and chives, mix thoroughly
- Check for flavour
- Cover and keep in the fridge. Use within two days

PARSNIP PATE   *Serves 2*

1 parsnip
1 dessertspoon rice flour
1 dessertspoon fresh dill or chives chopped

- Cook the parsnip
- Mash the parsnip in a bowl and add the dill or chives
- Add enough rice flour to make a pate consistency

Variation:
- **Use sweet potato or squash instead of parsnip**
- **Add onion and garlic instead of the herbs**
- **Use a little curry instead of herbs**

BASIC BEAN PATE *Serves 2-4*

225g / 8oz cooked haricot bean, butter bean or chick pea
1 dessertspoon olive oil
Juice 1/2 lemon
Salt and pepper

- Blend all the ingredients in a food processor or mash with a potato masher
- Add any of the variations below or one of your choice
- Keep covered in the fridge (no longer than three days) or freeze in little pots, taking out when required, defrost by placing in the fridge overnight

Variations:
- Garlic – add 1 - 2 cloves of crushed garlic
- Roasted garlic – roast by placing the whole garlic bulb in the oven, 190C/gas 5 for about 20-30 minutes or until the garlic is soft. Take out and cool.
  Squeeze the garlic from the bulbs and add to the paté.
- Chopped fresh herbs of your choice
- Curry powder or organic curry paste
- Chilli fresh or powdered to taste
- Spring onions finely chopped

SMOKED MACKEREL PATE *Serves 2*

1 smoked mackerel
1tbs cream cheese
Juice 1/2 lemon
1tbs fresh dill chopped

- Take the flesh from the mackerel, ensuring you take out all the bones
- Put the fish, cream cheese, lemon juice and dill into a food processor, blend until smooth, or use a fork to mash the fish first, then add the other ingredients and mix together
- Put into individual dishes, decorate with a little dill and slice of lemon

IDEAS OF MEALS

BREAKFASTS

• Organic porridge, sweeten with honey, organic maple syrup, dried fruit or fresh fruit. This porridge can be made from oats, rice flakes or quinoa flakes

• Make muesli with one or all of the above flakes. Soak a bowl of flakes overnight in natural live yoghurt; this makes it nice and creamy. In the morning add coconut, dried fruit, seeds, nuts and fresh fruit.

• Pancakes stuffed with fruits and yoghurt

• Organic puffed rice, millet or corn (available from health food stores), this doesn't taste of very much, so put it into a container and add coconut, seeds, dried fruit, nuts.

• Toasted oats (page 107)

• Fruit with natural live yoghurt

• Smoothie made from fruits, natural live yoghurt and pure juice if wished, blend in a liquidizer.

• Homemade popcorn, either plain or toasted (page 108)

• Eggs, tomatoes and herring cakes (page 30)

• Omelette, add grated carrot, watercress, cooked potato, grilled bacon, sprouted pulses, or something of your choice

LUNCHES

• Homemade soups (see soup section)

• Salads (see salad section)

• Pancake wraps (filling of your choice)

• Rice, millet, quinoa, pasta or rice noodle salads. Add raw vegetables, roasted vegetables, avocado pear, etc. Vary the dressings

- Fingers of raw vegetables with humus or homemade pates (see Miscellaneous section)
- Natural live yoghurt with fresh fruits and seeds

- Leftover main meal with salad

- Jacket potato with a filling, for example, humus, avocado pear, lentils or beans, fish, roasted vegetables, ratatouille or one of your choice

DINNER

- Stir fries with either beans, fish, tofu, meat or nuts Flavour with herbs, garlic, ginger and bouillon

- Roast meals with meat, nut loaf or lentil or bean loaf and homemade gravy (see sauce section)

- Casseroles with either bean, lentil or meat

- Roasted root or Mediterranean vegetables served on rice, pasta, quinoa or millet

- Homemade burgers made from meat, beans, lentils or tofu

- Homemade fish cakes

- Risotto with either beans, vegetables, fish, seafood, nuts or meat

- Curries made with either beans, lentils, meat, tofu, fish, nuts or eggs

- Omelettes with vegetables or salad

- Fish

- Jacket potatoes with various fillings for example; hummus, homemade baked beans, fish, lentils, ratatouille, avocado pear, roasted vegetables etc

- Large salads

- Pancakes stuffed

- Stuffed vegetables

- Vegetable crumble

- Vegetables in a white sauce served on rice, millet, quinoa or pasta

- Spaghetti bolognaise

- Tuna Au-Gratin

- Quiche with or without a pastry base

- Scotch eggs

- Sweet and sour vegetables served on rice, millet or Quinoa

- Cottage pie made from meat or lentils

DESSERTS

- Fresh fruits

- Yoghurt and fruit whip

- Pancakes stuffed with fruits or berries

- Fruit crumbles

- Homemade rice pudding

- Jelly

- Fruit with custard (natural custard powder available from health food shops)

SUPPLIERS LIST

LOCAL HEALTH FOOD SHOPS

Healthy Pulses: Plymouth City Centre – Tel: 01752 261669
Plympton Ridgeway – Tel: 01752 341335
Exeter – Tel: 01392 250552
Web site: www.healthypulses.co.uk

Natures Larder Ivybridge – Tel: 01752 894197
Web site: www.natureslarder.co.uk

Natural Way Paignton – Tel: 01803 665529
Web site: naturalwayhealth.co.uk

Kilworthy Kapers Tavistock – Tel: 01822 615039

Green Life Totnes – Tel: 01803 866738

ORGANIC VEGETABLE BOX SCHEMES

Riverford Organic Vegetables Limited
Tel: 01803 762720
Web site: www.riverford.co.uk

Rod and Ben Organic Vegetables
Tel: 01392 833833
Web site: www.rodandbens.com

Farmers Markets: Search Engine: "farmers markets" and "your area"

JT's products Email: nuttyjules45@hotmail.com
Web site: www.jtnutrition.co.uk
Seed Mix for snacking or adding to food
Carob treats with and without sugar
Hemp French Dressing
Linseed Oil Dressing
Three day sprout mix
Six day sprout mix
Candida Seed Mix for snacking or adding to food

INDEX